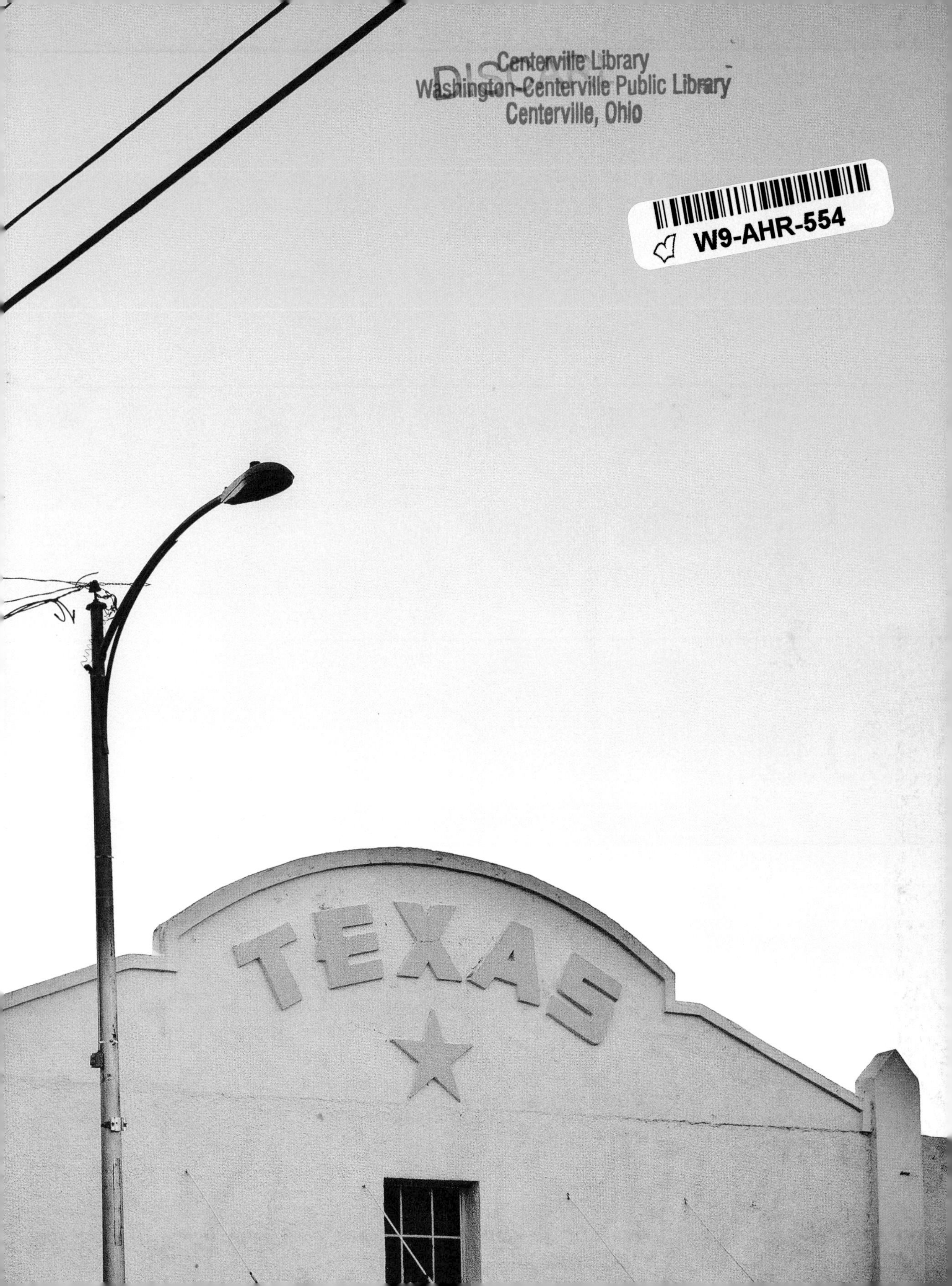
TEXAS

BQ

BY JONAS CRAMBY

CONT

ENTS

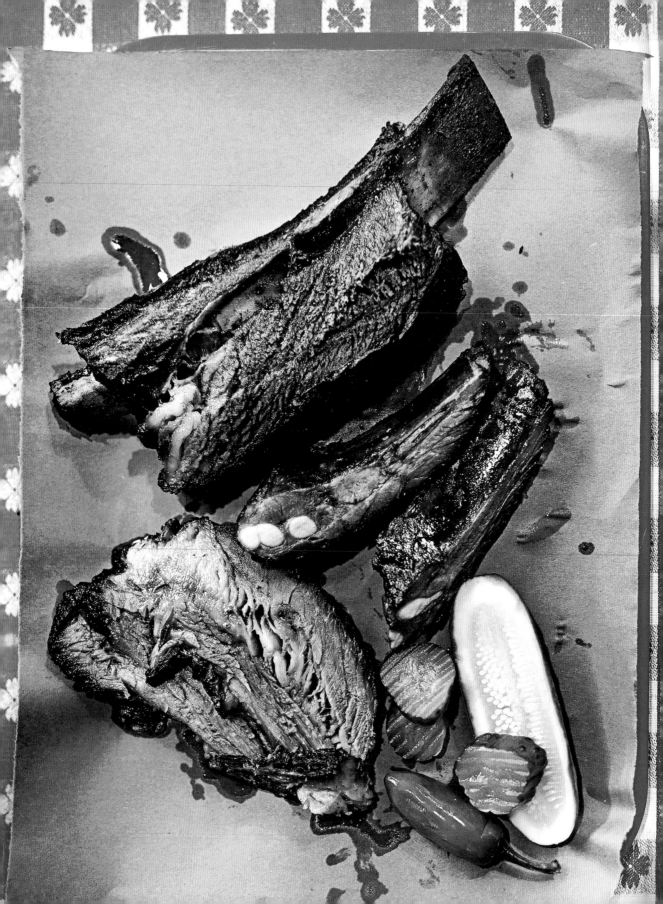

WHAT IS BARBECUE?

Sometimes there can be some confusion with regard to the concept of the barbecue. Is it a special spice or outdoor grill? Or is it simply a synonym for grilling? The answer to all these questions is no. So what is barbecue then?

I'll start with the long answer.

If traditional grilling means to quickly cook a piece of meat at a high temperature, barbecue works just the opposite way: here, it's slow cooking at low temperatures. Barbecue, you could say, is simply like discovering that your outdoor grill also has an oven function. This method of cooking meat has several benefits. On average, meat loses between 25 and 30 per cent in weight during cooking, so the low, even heat in a barbecue helps the meat to retain a lot more of its juices. The meat is record-breakingly juicy, and at the same time it develops the dark, crispy crust that's called bark. This bark works a bit like a perfectly grilled chicken skin and adds crispiness, stickiness, chewiness and wonderful caramel flavours to the juicy, smoky meat.

The slow cooking process also breaks down the collagen in cheap and tough, but often a lot more flavour-rich, cuts of meat. These become fantastically tender, and at the same time, the meat's natural fat has got time to slowly melt and moisturise the meat from within. When the source of heat is wood, you automatically get an unbeatable flavour enhancer in the form of smoke – smoother and more comforting than the smell of granddad's pipe tobacco.

But it's not only tastier to smoke-barbecue one's meat – it's also cosier. To stand and guard a slowly smouldering barbecue grill with an ice-cold beer in your hand on a warm summer afternoon is one of life's simple pleasures. You get time to ponder while fiddling with the fire, and you will soon feel how the smell of the smoke, meat and spices slowly transform into something so much larger than the sum of its parts. And that's when your loved ones start gathering around.

Since the start of human civilisation, barbecuing has been an opportunity to gather around the fire to hang out, drink beer, listen to music, talk rubbish and wait for it to be ready at some point.

To put it simply, eating perfectly barbecued meat together with the ones you love is at the same time an expression of culture, bodily function, an act of love, and, above all, an opportunity to throw a party.

And that was the long answer.

So what then is the short one?

Well, barbecue is smoke, meat and love.

JONAS CRAMBY

 Love on a plastic tray from Black's BBQ in Lockhart, Texas.

Part 1

BBQ
BASICS

CHOOSING THE RIGHT
SMOKER

The biggest investment for the aspiring pitmaster is without a doubt the smoker. So, which one should you go ahead and buy? Well, I don't know. It depends on everything from your budget to how many people you want to be able to feed. Personally, I have a kamado grill that I love as much as if it were a pet.

KETTLE GRILL

A common kettle grill with a lid is often the introductory model for the barbecue novice. The pros are that it's cheap and easy to get hold of, as well as easy to use for two-zone grilling (when you have to change between indirect and direct heat quickly). The cons are that it's difficult to maintain a constant heat and that you won't fit a lot of meat in it. To cook with indirect heat on a kettle grill, place the charcoal in one half of the grill and in the other half, place the meat on a rack with an aluminium pan filled with water underneath. Since the only way you're able to control the heat is how much charcoal you use, it's important that you don't use too much. About 8-10 pieces is normally enough to keep the heat at around 115°C/239°F. Add more charcoal when needed and don't lift the lid too often.

OIL DRUM GRILL

The step up from a kettle grill is the oil drum grill – which you can either make yourself or buy for around £100 ($160) at your local DIY or home improvement store. The pros are that it's cheap, large, as well as easy to use for two-zone grilling (when you have to transfer between indirect and direct heat quickly). The con is that it's difficult to maintain a consistent heat. To cook with indirect heat, place the charcoal in one half of the grill and in the other half, place the meat on a rack with an aluminium pan filled with water underneath. Since the only way you're able to control the heat is how much

charcoal you use, it's important that you don't use too much. About 15-20 pieces is normally enough to keep the heat at around 115°C/239°F. Add more coal when needed and don't lift the lid too often.

BULLET SMOKER

A bullet smoker looks like an upright drum grill and is normally found in DIY or home improvement stores for a fairly cheap price. The pro with this model is that it's made for barbecuing, so it's fairly easy to maintain the heat for a long time. The con is that if you need to use two-zone grilling (when you have to change between indirect and direct heat quickly), you will need a separate grill on the side – or use your chimney starter as a turbo grill (see p.93). To cook with indirect heat using a bullet smoker, place the charcoal in the bottom of the grill, then place a divider with a pan of water over the top, and place the rack with the meat on top of that. You control the temperature by adjusting different valves to increase or decrease the supply of oxygen.

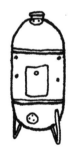

The smoker at Smitty's Market in Lockhart in Texas is an ancient closed pit that is only lit with wood from post oak. Not for the home-griller perhaps.

KAMADO GRILL

A kamado grill is a Japanese ceramic grill that's become incredibly popular in barbecuing circles. The pros are that it's very easy to control the temperature and since the ceramics isolate the heat, it's usually enough to get it up to the right temperature once and then it will last for the rest of the day. The kamado grill is also very dense, which means that the steam stays inside the grill and that the meat juices stay inside the meat. When you don't want to barbecue, it can also be used as a normal outdoor grill as well as a stone oven. The cons are that it's expensive and if you need to use two-zone grilling (when you have to change between indirect and direct heat quickly), you will need a separate grill on the side - or use your chimney starter as a turbo grill (see p.93). To cook with indirect heat, place the charcoal on the bottom of the grill, place a divider with a pan of water over the top, and put the rack with the meat on top of that. You control the temperature by adjusting different valves to increase or decrease the supply of oxygen.

OFFSET SMOKER

An offset smoker is the archetypal barbecue grill and looks like an oil drum grill but with a chimney and a small fireplace attached to its side. The pros with this type of grill is that it's easy to maintain a consistent temperature, you can use both charcoal and firewood as a heat source, and cook large quantities of food at the same time - almost all offset smokers are used in competitions and catering. The cons are that it's often expensive, plus it's so difficult to control the

amount of smoke when using firewood that this function is hardly practical at all for the home-griller. To cook with indirect heat, light a fire in the fireplace using either wood or charcoal. From the fireplace, the smoke is led through the drum and then out through the chimney. The meat rests on a rack inside the drum, with an aluminium pan filled with water underneath. You control the temperature by adjusting different valves to increase or decrease the supply of oxygen.

GAS GRILL

Even though you'll probably get bullied by other home-grillers, you can actually use most gas grills for barbecuing. The pros are that it's easy to control the heat at the turn of a button, and it's also easy to use for two-zone grilling (when you have to change between indirect and direct heat quickly). The cons are that gas grills are expensive and lame. To cook with indirect heat, simply turn off the gas burners in the section of the grill where the meat is placed. Some gas grills have a built-in box for wood smoking chips - if not, you can probably buy one in your local DIY or home improvement store or make one yourself using an aluminium roasting tray with holes in it.

WHAT TOOLS DO I NEED?

There's umpteen grilling accessories to buy for those who are interested, but remember that most of them will just sit in the garage collecting dust. There are, however, a few things that you actually need to achieve an ultimate grilling result. Here's a little shopping list.

STEAK THERMOMETER
After a good grill, a steak thermometer is the first thing you will need to invest in. It doesn't matter if it's a hi-tech stick connected to your smartphone or your grandmother's old analogue one – as long as you can measure the inside temperature of the meat, you will eliminate all the guessing and you can achieve that perfect barbecue result (almost) every time.

OVEN THERMOMETER
Since the barbecue-principle is based on low heat for a long time, it's important that the temperature in the grill never, not even for a second, exceeds that of the recipe – or the meat will immediately lose its juices and become dry and boring. Many grills are already fitted with a thermometer, but if yours doesn't have one or if it doesn't seem up to scratch, a separate oven thermometer will set you back about £5 ($8) and can be found in most department stores.

CHIMNEY STARTER
If you are grilling with charcoal, there's probably no reason to use lighter fluid. It's expensive, dangerous, bad for the environment and will give your meat a foul taste. A chimney starter, on the other hand, won't run out, lights your coal before you have time to blink, and can be used as an extra turbo grill (see p.93). Buy one now.

BARBECUE SAUCE BRUSH
Since the brushes you buy from supermarkets are sized for brushing icing onto cupcakes, it's a good idea to buy paintbrushes from a DIY or home improvement store. Do, however, buy ones with natural bristles so you don't get melted plastic bristles all over the meat. Not nice.

WORK GLOVES
Grill tongs and barbecue forks are great, but did you know that the world's best grilling tools are already pre-fitted at the end of your arms? In fact, I very rarely use anything else but my hands when I cook on a grill – but in order not to burn them, I put on a pair of heat-resistant work gloves (which I, of course, keep clean and only use for the barbecue).

GARDEN RECLINER
The fourth most important barbecue ingredient after meat, spice and smoke is patience. So buy a cheap garden recliner at the nearest petrol station, preferably one with a cup holder on the armrest. Perhaps with some cool flames. And when someone asks you to move, you can calmly stay seated and say 'sorry, keeping an eye on that one' and nod towards the grill. Perfect.

WOOD AND SMOKING CHIPS

Our love for the taste of meat cooked with the help of burning wood is perhaps not so strange: that's how we prepared all our food before some wet bureaucratic type invented the electric stove a hundred years ago. Some researchers even think that it was in fact the grilled meat that gave us the extra energy needed to develop larger brains than the other slightly dim-witted animals.

CHARCOAL, FIREWOOD OR BRIQUETTES?

Firewood made from oak is the classic choice if you want to create an authentic Texas barbecue. It burns slowly and gives the food a natural smoky flavour. It is, however, not practical for most home-grillers since using firewood requires an offset smoker and large quantities of food to grill. Plus, if you don't want to oversmoke the meat, you will have to leave the wood until most of it has burned down to the embers - a lot of hassle. So, for most people a bag of good charcoal together with some wood smoking chips is the best option. Coal briquettes, on the other hand, might burn for longer, but contain binders and chemicals that can give meat a chemical taste.

HOW TO LIGHT THE GRILL

There are lots of different ways to light your barbecue. The best is to invest in a chimney starter. You won't get any unwanted flavours from the lighting paraphernalia and you will get a better charring on the coals. A chimney starter is also easy to use: fill with charcoal, stuff some newspaper underneath and light up. Feed with paper for about 5 minutes until you have a batch of perfect burning coal that you just spread out over the grill. A chimney starter is extra important when barbecuing, as you might need to add extra charcoal as you go.

HOW MANY WOOD SMOKING CHIPS?

Once you have some nice charcoal, you will need to add wood smoking chips to flavour the meat. About two to three handfuls are normally enough but as with everything else, it's a question of taste. If you use too little the flavour will be too bland, and if you use too much you can end up with something tasting like petrol. Sprinkle some wood smoking chips directly on top of the burning charcoal and the rest along the edges to allow them to burn slowly and release the smoke for as long as possible. If you are grilling with charcoal use smoking chips made out of larger pieces of wood, while for the gas griller use finer wood chips.

WHICH KIND OF WOOD SMOKING CHIPS SHOULD I USE?

They say that when a barbecue is really well made, you should be able to taste the flavour of the individual tree that cooked it. And that's actually how it is, just like with the manufacturing of wine, the wood is an extremely important part of really good barbecue - so don't use just any old chipboard. Here's a little guide to which type of wood goes well with which type of meat. Personally, I like the sweet smokiness of the apple wood for most things, perhaps with some extra hickory or mesquite for increasing the smoke level a tad when cooking beef, for example.

LITTLE SMOKING WOOD GUIDE

WOOD	FLAVOUR	SUITABLE FOR
Apple	Mild, sweet and fruity	Pork, poultry and beef
Cherry	Distinct, sweet and fruity	Pork and poultry
Hickory	Strong and smoky	Pork, poultry and beef
Mesquite	Strong and super-smoky	Beef
Oak	Distinct and smoky	Beef, chicken and fish
Pecan	Earthy and distinct	Beef, chicken and fish

The wood storage behind Smitty's Market in Lockhart, Texas

TIPS AND TECHNIQUES

If baking is a science and cooking an art, barbecue is a craft. You will also need knowledge, experience and practise if you want to become really good at barbecuing. Here's a little help along the way.

The first thing every aspiring pitmaster needs to learn is how to control the temperature on the grill. All grills are different and as the temperature is the key to a successful result, you will need to know how to quickly decrease the heat when it's too hot and vice versa.

There are a lot of issues with our meat consumption but the two major ones are industrially manufactured meat and that we simply eat too much of it. So always buy good meat from happy animals and don't eat it too often. Nevertheless, a serendipitous side effect of the barbecue is that you will never want to eat nasty meat ever again.

Remember that all meat is individual. Two cuts of meat that appear the same can take different times to cook.

Therefore, regard the times and inside temperatures in this book as guidelines only. Is it not tender yet? Leave it for a bit longer.

Don't be afraid of what the Americans call 'the stall'. It means that the inside temperature rises steadily then suddenly stops at a certain degree and sticks, often for hours on end. When this happens, it's important not to panic, increase the heat or take the meat out too early.

To become a really competent pitmaster is a lifetime project. So after every completed grilling session, sit down with a beer, a notebook and a bunch of toothpicks, and contemplate the following: what can I improve for next time? What did I do right? And shall I grab another beer?

WHEN IS THE FOOD READY?*

CUT OF MEAT	WEIGHT	TIME	INSIDE TEMPERATURE
Baby back ribs	500g/1lb 2oz	About 4 hours	90°C/194°F
St Louis-style ribs	1kg/2¼lb	About 5 hours	90°C/194°F
Beef ribs	1.5kg/3¼lb	About 5-7 hours	82-87°C/179.6-188.6°F
Pork collar (neck), whole	4-6kg/8¾-13¼lb	18-20 hours	Pulled, 90°C/194°F; Sliced, 80°C/176°F
Pork collar (neck), cut	1kg/2¼lb	About 5-7 hours	Pulled, 90°C/194°F; Sliced, 80°C/176°F
Texas hot links	Standard sausage size	1-2 hours	73°C/163°F
Brisket, whole	6kg/13¼lb	About 12-16 hours	85-90°C/185-194°F
Whole chicken	1.5kg/3¼lb	About 2-3 hours	74°C/165°F

* Cooked using the barbecue method at between 110°C/230°F and 120°C/248°F.

Barbecue assistant taking a break at Snow's BBQ in Lexington, Texas.

BARBECUE IN THE OVEN, DOES IT WORK?

No. Or, yes. Or, like this: in an oven, you obviously won't get that smoky flavour or the magical bark that the meat gets when cooked using wood. At the same time, a closed grill that cooks the food with indirect heat is in principle just a primitive kind of outdoor oven, which means that all recipes in this book **can** be cooked indoors in the oven. Even if it, of course, isn't barbecuing.

RUBS

Forget marinades, grilling oils and glaze. The only thing you need to create a top-notch barbecue is a good rub and a tasty barbecue sauce. A rub is a carefully balanced spice mix that you gently pat into the meat and that then helps to create one of the most delicious components in a really good barbecue: the bark. Here are some varieties.

MAGIC DUST
The all-round rub from the legend Mark Mills.

100g/3½oz/scant 1 cup paprika
50g/2oz/scant ¼ cup salt
2 tbsp mustard powder
50g/2oz ground cumin
2 tbsp finely ground black pepper
50g/2oz garlic powder
2 tbsp cayenne pepper
50g/2oz/½ cup granulated sugar

Mix all the ingredients together and blend into a fine powder.

TEXAS RUB
A classic Texan rub.

100g/3½oz/scant 1 cup paprika
100g/3½oz/⅓ cup salt
100g/3½oz/1 cup black pepper
1 tsp cayenne pepper

Mix all the ingredients together and blend into a fine powder.

REAL TEXAS RUB
The most archetypal Texan rub of them all; best suited for beef.

100g/3½oz/⅓ cup salt
100g/3½oz/1 cup black pepper

Mix the salt and pepper together and blend into a fine powder.

RED RUB
Red rub for chicken and pork.

100g/3½oz/scant 1 cup paprika
2 tbsp brown sugar
2 tbsp granulated sugar
2 tbsp salt
3 tsp black pepper
2 tsp cayenne pepper
2 tsp mustard powder
2 tsp garlic powder
2 tsp onion powder

Mix all the ingredients together and blend into a fine powder.

ANGEL DUST
– JONAS CRAMBY'S SIGNATURE RUB
Crushing the spices yourself means a bit more effort, but also a bit more flavour.

1 tbsp mustard seeds
1 tbsp fennel seeds
100g/3½oz/scant 1 cup Hungarian paprika
50g/2oz/scant ¼ cup salt
50g/2oz/scant ¼ cup salt ground cumin
2 tbsp brown sugar
2 tbsp granulated sugar
2 tbsp kodjokaro (Korean chilli powder used for kimchi, among other things, and that can be found in Asian food stores)
1 tbsp finely ground black pepper

Toast the mustard seeds and fennel seeds in a dry pan. When they start to smell nice, crush or blend them into a fine powder. Add the other spices and blend again.

HOW TO MAKE YOUR OWN
SIGNATURE RUB

Every pitmaster worthy of the (somewhat silly) name has, of course, their own signature rub. And you'd like one too, right? Now unfortunately you can't just come up with any mixture. There are a few tried and tested ingredients and proportions that you should stick to as a beginner if you don't want the meat to taste like the inside of an old hat from a car boot sale.

STEP 1

START WITH 100G/3½ OZ/SCANT 1 CUP PAPRIKA
The base for most rubs is paprika. It gives a good flavour and a beautiful colour. You can, however, choose whether you'd like a sweet, hot or smoky variety. It could be bought from your local food store or from a Hungarian you have palled up with at the motorway services outside some random town. You decide; it's your signature rub.

STEP 2

ADD 50G/2OZ/SCANT ¾ CUP SALT
When the choice of paprika is over and done with, it's time to add the salt. Here you have a choice, sea salt or perhaps pink Himalayan salt? With or without iodine? I don't know, you decide (but if you use salt flakes you will have to finely grind it first).

STEP 3

ADD 0–100G/3½OZ/½ CUP GRANULATED SUGAR
Now for the sweet part. You can use white, brown or muscovado sugar - or a combination (but not stevia). If you want a sweeter rub, add some more sugar. Less sweet: less sugar of course. Just remember that sweet rubs burn easier.

STEP 4

ADD 1–2 TBSP CHILLI POWDER
What would salt and sweet be without spicy? Exactly. So of course we will want some chilli in our signature rub. Here you have some choices. Do you want smoky chipotle, standard chilli, dried ancho, black pepper or cayenne? All you have to remember is that if you use a whole dried chilli or chilli flakes you will need to blitz them in a spice mill until you have a fine powder.

STEP 5

ADD OTHER SPICES
Now when the rub base is done, you're free to go crazy with pretty much any spices you like. Experiment! Just remember not to use any wet stuff (so, garlic powder instead of garlic and so on) and that everything needs to be ground to a fine powder. The rub should be fine enough to run through a saltshaker.

STEP 6

BLEND
When your rub recipe is sorted, finish it off by mixing it all in a blender. This is necessary partly so that the rub is mixed together properly and partly to make sure that everything really gets pulverised. Pour into a saltshaker, sprinkle over the meat and start barbecuing. If you're not entirely happy, start again. When the rub is tried, tested and done, the only remaining thing is to name it, perhaps Name Nameson's Super Rub? And then never breathe a word to anyone about how you made it. Okay?

BBQ SAUCES

A barbecue sauce is, in contrast to common belief, not a marinade. It's a sauce you ladle over the cooked meat or at the most leave to caramelise over the meat right at the end of the cooking process. It's also, if you make it right, as if you have captured the sound of children's laughter inside an old ketchup jar. Here are a few of my favourite varieties.

BASIC BARBECUE SAUCE

A hot, sweet-spicy barbecue sauce that's a great match with both pork and chicken as well as beef.

1 brown onion, finely chopped
6 garlic cloves, finely chopped
2 tbsp olive oil
1 tsp ground cumin
50ml/2fl oz/scant 1/4 cup balsamic vinegar
100g/3½oz/½ cup brown sugar
50ml/2fl oz/scant 1/4 cup Japanese soy sauce
1 tbsp Worcestershire sauce
100ml/3½fl oz/scant ½ cup tomato
    passata (strained tomatoes)
2 dried chillies, eg ancho

Sauté the onion and garlic in the oil with the cumin. When the onion starts to soften, deglaze the pan by adding the balsamic vinegar and leave to simmer for a couple of minutes. Add the brown sugar, soy sauce and Worcestershire sauce as well as the tomato passata (strained tomatoes). Remove the stalk and seeds from the chillies, then drop them into the sauce and leave to simmer gently for 10 minutes or until nice and sticky. Blend into a smooth sauce.

HIPSTER COFFEE BARBECUE SAUCE

This (even tastier) variation of the signature sauce of Franklin BBQ in Austin goes perfectly well with both pork and beef.

1 brown onion, finely chopped
6 garlic cloves, finely chopped
2 tsp corn oil
1 tsp salt
1 tsp dried oregano
½ tsp ground cumin
2 tsp cider vinegar
250ml/9fl oz/generous 1 cup strong hipster
    coffee or ordinary black coffee
50g/2oz/1/4 cup brown sugar
2 tbsp granulated sugar
250ml/9fl oz/generous 1 cup tomato
    passata (strained tomatoes)
2-4 dried chillies, eg ancho

Sauté the onion and garlic in the oil with the salt, oregano and cumin. When the onion starts to soften, deglaze the pan by adding the cider vinegar and leave to simmer for a couple of minutes. Add the coffee, sugars and tomato passata (strained tomatoes). Remove the stalk and seeds from the chillies, then drop them into the sauce and leave to simmer gently for 10 minutes or until nice and sticky. Blend into a smooth sauce and leave on the heat to reduce a little.

BOURBON BARBECUE SAUCE

Booze or barbecue sauce? Why choose?

1 brown onion, finely chopped
3 garlic cloves, finely chopped
2 tbsp butter
200ml/7fl oz/generous 3/4 cup bourbon
200ml/7fl oz/generous 3/4 cup tomato
    passata (strained tomatoes)
50g/2oz/1/4 cup brown sugar
2 dried chillies, eg ancho
salt and freshly ground black pepper

Sauté the onion and garlic in the butter. When the onion starts to soften, deglaze the pan by adding the bourbon and leave to simmer for a couple of minutes. Add the tomato passata (strained tomatoes) and sugar.

Remove the stalk and seeds from the chillies, then drop them into the sauce and leave to simmer gently for 10 minutes or until nice and sticky. Season and blend into a smooth sauce.

TEXAS MOPPING SAUCE
A classic sauce that can also be used for brushing the meat during cooking.

1 brown onion, finely chopped
6 garlic cloves, finely chopped
2 tbsp corn oil
1 tsp salt
½ tsp fennel seeds
½ tsp cumin seeds
2 tbsp brown sugar
200ml/7fl oz/generous ¾ cup cider vinegar
400ml/14fl oz/1¾ cups tomato passata
   (strained tomatoes)
1 tbsp Worcestershire sauce
2–4 dried chillies, eg ancho

Sauté the onion and garlic in the oil with the salt, fennel and cumin seeds. Add the sugar and cider vinegar and leave to simmer. Add the tomato passata and Worcestershire sauce. Remove the stalk and seeds from the chillies, then drop them into the sauce and leave to simmer for 10 minutes or until nice and sticky. Blend into a smooth sauce.

CAROLINE HOT 'N' NASTY
In the Southern states, they prefer sour, thin barbecue sauces like this one.

200ml/7fl oz/generous ¾ cup cider vinegar
50ml/2fl oz/scant ¼ cup distilled vinegar (12%)
1 tbsp granulated sugar
1 tbsp salt
6 fresh chillies, eg habañero, halved

Mix the cider vinegar, distilled vinegar, 150ml/5fl oz/⅔ cup water, the sugar and salt together. Once the sugar and salt have dissolved, pour the mixture into a nice bottle and add the halved chillies.

MAPLE MUSTARD BARBECUE SAUCE
A simple barbecue sauce for pork and chicken.

100ml/3½fl oz/scant ½ cup maple syrup
2½ tbsp wholegrain Dijon mustard
1 garlic clove, crushed
salt and freshly ground black pepper
½ lemon

Mix the maple syrup, mustard and crushed garlic together. Add salt, pepper and lemon.

MANGO HABAÑERO BARBECUE SAUCE
A fruity hot sauce for pork and chicken.

½ brown onion, finely chopped
2 garlic cloves, finely chopped
1 tbsp oil
50g/2oz/¼ cup brown sugar
50g/2oz/scant ¼ cup honey
1 tbsp yellow mustard powder
50ml/2fl oz/scant ¼ cup cider vinegar
1 mango, peeled, stoned and chopped
200ml/7fl oz/generous ¾ cup tomato
   passata (strained tomatoes)
½ tbsp Worcestershire sauce
1 lime
1–2 fresh chillies, eg habañero
salt and freshly ground black pepper

Sauté the onion and garlic in the oil. When the onion starts to soften, add the sugar, honey, mustard powder, and cider vinegar. Leave to simmer for a couple of minutes. Add the mango, passata, Worcestershire sauce and squeeze over the lime. Remove the stalk and seeds from the chilli, then add to the sauce and leave to simmer gently for 10 minutes or until nice and sticky. Season and blend into a smooth sauce.

The secret barbecue sauce at City Market in Luling, Texas.

Part 2

CEN

The first stop on our barbecue journey is the area around Austin in central Texas. Here, only the toughest, cheapest cuts from the cow are used and rarely any other spices than salt and pepper. Despite this, the meat from most of the area's many barbecue places tastes almost always as if a piece of heaven has fallen down from above and landed on your disposable plate.

Even though several other American states claim to have the world's tastiest barbecue, you will really find the best one in Texas. And this is not only empty Texas bragging, because the state's proximity to both the American South and Mexico – as well as its varied history made up of Central European immigrants, cowboys and Indians – have created a completely unique cuisine like nothing else in the world. A kind of delicate fusion between German smoked deli meat, Mexican barbacoa and sticky-sauce South State barbecue. And that's just why Texas has the world's best barbecue: because where the other famous barbecue states have only one local cooking style, Texas has them all.

However, when you talk about typical Texas barbecue, it's mostly the type they cook in central Texas that is referred to. A significant number of Germans and other Central Europeans immigrated to small towns like Elgin, Lockhart, Luling, Round Rock and Taylor in the area around Austin in the nineteenth century. They brought with them their home countries' food culture and a number of German meat markets, popped up. In these German meat markets they smoked meat and sausages like in the old country, but with the new country's produce, and these were places where grafters and cowboys could get a tasty, quick, cheap and filling meal. Although the German immigrants didn't think of their food as barbecue, this is what the locals started calling it and the name stuck.

A lot of these old meat markets are still standing today, wonderfully permeated by centuries of smoke, and the same rules still apply now as back then: they open at 11am and serve the meat they left to cook in the enormous grills the night before until it runs out. There's mostly beef on the menu, only seasoned with salt and pepper, and simply served on a piece of red butcher paper. To accompany the meat there's pickles, onion, jalapeños, white tin loaf, and if there's any barbecue sauce at all, it's served on the side. For in Central Texas, it's all about the quality of the meat. In the following chapters, you will learn how to prepare your meat just as well using your home grill, because from now on you don't have to go to Texas to find the world's best barbecue.

Black's BBQ in Lockhart, Texas. Lockhart also goes under the name of 'the barbecue capital of the world' because of all the remaining old beautiful German meat markets.

B.B.Q. CAPITOL OF TEXAS

FAMOUS
BLACK'S
BARBECUE OF
LOCKHART

est. 1932

Gary P. Nunn

IT'S A TEXAS THING.

LONE STAR

SINCE 1978

CERTIFIED
ANGUS BEEF®
BRAND

NOT Angus. NOT Black Angus.
It's the Certified Angus Beef® brand.

BRISKET

The national dish of Texas is without a doubt brisket – slowly barbecued beef brisket. It is, however, a notoriously difficult cut of meat to get right. If the brisket isn't cooked enough it gets tough and inedible, and if it's cooked for too long it gets dry and boring. When you manage to cook it to perfection, however, something supernatural occurs, magic that makes the end result taste so incredibly much more than the sum of its parts. A really good brisket is smooth, tender and buttery under the crispy, salty bark surface – at the same time as still being so juicy that it wobbles like a beer belly when you throw it down on the chopping board.

BRISKET FACTS

In central Texas, the holy barbecue trinity is made up of brisket, hot links and pork ribs. But greatest of them all is, of course, brisket. This cut of meat is, contrary to popular belief, not the same thing as the Swedish 'nötbringa'. While the Swedish cut is made out of the whole front part of the cow's chest, the brisket is the thick meaty part at the bottom of the chest. In Sweden 'nötbringa' is often eaten salted and in pieces – which, if you want to barbecue brisket, is wrong. Instead, ask your butcher for a whole, fresh brisket with the fat cap (fatty side of the brisket) still attached. If they don't have this, a butcher can usually order one in for you.

SERVES 6

1 whole (about 6kg/13¼lb) brisket
real Texas rub (see p.21)
hickory wood smoking chips
1 beer
foil

A brisket is covered in a fat cap (fatty side of the brisket), and if it's too thick the end result will be too fatty, and if it's too thin the meat will be too dry. Trim the fat down so that you're left with ½–1cm/¼–½in fat all around. It's easiest to do this with a sharp knife and while the meat is cold. If you see any sinews or silver skin, remove these too. Between the point and the flat, there is also a large rind of fat that you can remove. Pat the meat with the rub and leave until it is at room temperature.

Prepare your grill for indirect cooking (see p.13). When you have a consistent temperature of somewhere between 115°C/239°F and 120°C/248°F, throw in a couple of handfuls of wood smoking chips and place the meat on the rack – fatty side up and the thick side closest to the heat (depending on which kind of grill you have). Start barbecuing. Allow for between 60 and 75 minutes per 500g/1lb 2oz of meat, which means about 12 hours for a brisket of 6kg/13¼lb.

This is when the tricky bit starts because although you don't want to take a peak too often as the heat will escape (a consistent heat is the key for a successful brisket), you will have to keep an eye on the meat so that it doesn't dry out or get too dark. Pour a cold beer into a spray flask and be prepared to spray if the surface of the meat seems dry. When the meat has turned a beautiful mahogany colour, after about 6 hours, it's time to wrap it in foil. Hardcore home-grillers use waxed butcher paper or baking parchment – but if you want a juicier result, and if your guests are arriving soon, use foil, which speeds up the process. Leave until the inside temperature has reached 85°C/185°F – about 6 hours, the meat should still feel wobbly and soft.

Rest the meat still wrapped up for 1 hour before carving. Serve with finely sliced white onion, your choice of pickles (see p.104), your choice of barbecue sauce (see p.24), white sourdough bread (see p.98) or your choice of sides (see p.94).

HOW TO MAKE A TIPSY TEXAN

Since brisket is such a large cut of meat, there's a great chance you will end up with lots of leftovers after barbecuing one. You could, of course, eat it cold from the fridge, use it for the world's most delicious hotpot (hotchpotch), or do as Franklin BBQ in Austin and make the super-sandwich Tipsy Texan - that comes with so much filling it almost tips over. This is easy: place sliced dill pickles on the bottom half of a ce-mita and chop up an embarrassingly large amount of warm brisket that you will then try to balance on top of the bun. Put sliced Texas hot links on top and finish off with an ample dollop of classic coleslaw. Put the other half of the bun on top. Eat. Feel the guilt. Eat some more. The first five people who make a Tipsy Texan from the recipe in this book, upload a picture on Instagram and tag me (jonascramby) then they will get my next cookbook for free with a red bow attached. I promise.

THE POINT

THE FLAT

ANATOMY OF THE BRISKET

When you order brisket in barbecue restaurants, they often ask 'moist or lean?' and what they mean with this is simply from which side of the brisket would you like your meat. A brisket is made up of two parts: 'the point' which is the thicker part with more marbled fat and 'the flat' which is the thinner part containing the lean meat. Which one you prefer is a matter of taste. To ensure both sides are ready at the same time, it's important that you choose a brisket where the flat is as thick as possible. It's also important that you consider these two parts when it's time to carve the meat. You do this by first slicing the flat against the meat fibres into about 3mm/⅛in thick slices. When you reach the point, turn the brisket 90 degrees and divide in half. These two pieces you then slice into about 6mm/¼in thick slices against the meat fibres. The thickest half is the best bit, so save it for someone you like, and the end bit of the thicker half is called 'the burnt end' and is the tastiest part of the whole cow. So you will, of course, eat that yourself. You deserve it.

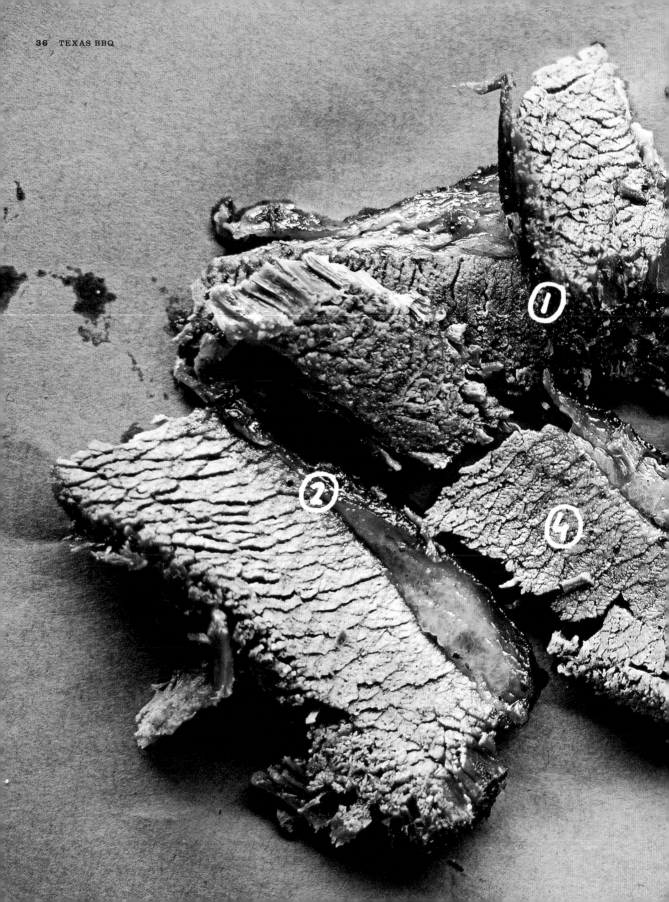

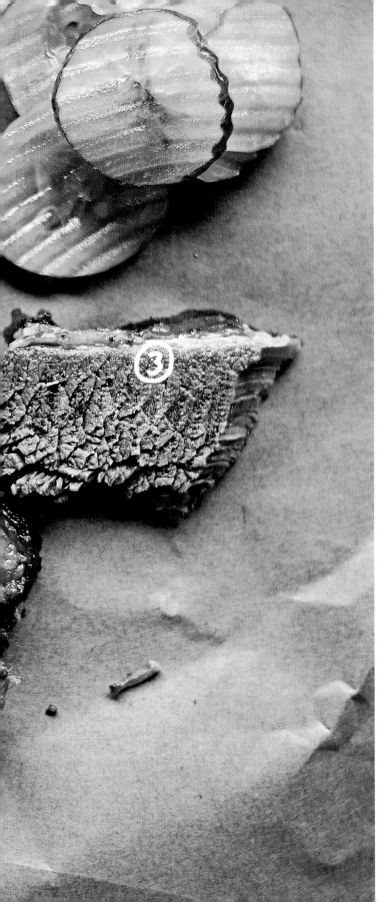

HOW TO RECOGNISE A PERFECTLY COOKED BIT OF BRISKET

THE BARK
The crispy black crust that is formed around the meat should not only taste of smoke, salt and freshly ground black pepper, but should also taste fantastic due to the maillard reaction – the chemical process that occurs when heat meets the meat proteins – and pure and unadulterated flavour bliss appears.

THE CARAMEL
If the meat has been exposed to enough smoke, there's also another chemical process occurring where the meat, together with the rub, merge into a sticky, almost sweet crust called 'caramel'. It's this caramel that gets stuck on your fingers and makes you walk around with a brown, sticky sheepish smile on your lips for the rest of the day. This sticky surface some-times also forms into little crispy clusters called 'candy', and you're a real jammy one if you happen to get one of these in your meat portion.

THE SMOKE RING
Directly underneath the bark, there should be a clearly visible pinkish-red line if the brisket is cooked correctly (just like with any other meat). This smoke ring indicates that the meat has been exposed to the right amount of smoke and that you haven't cheated by using an electric smoke machine or the oven.

THE INSIDE
When you cook meat slow 'n' low, the fat will slowly melt and moisturise the meat from within, which results in a juicy, flavourful, almost buttery meat. This method also means that the small amount of fat that remains tastes so delicious and has such a nice texture that you'll happily munch that down too – even if finding nasty bits of fat in your lunch beef would normally make you gag.

In central Texas, they prefer their ribs simpler than in other places in the US. Not as many spices, no trimmings and absolutely no sticky barbecue sauce. The meat should, however, feature a beautiful red smoke ring, be juicy with a dark, crispy bark and a deep, deep smoky flavour.

SERVES 6

3 whole racks (about 2.5kg/5½ lb) of pork
   spare ribs
Texas rub (see p.21)
hickory or apple wood smoking chips
foil
100ml/3½ fl oz/scant ½ cup cider vinegar
100ml/3½ fl oz/scant ½ cup beer
5 garlic cloves, half crushed

Remove the silver-coloured membrane on the back of the ribs. Sprinkle with the rub, and remember that despite the name 'rub' you shouldn't rub it, but rather pat it in gently. Leave to marinate in the fridge for 1–4 hours.

Prepare your grill for indirect cooking (see p.13). When you have a consistent temperature of somewhere between 115°C/239°F and 120°C/248°F, throw in a couple of handfuls of wood smoking chips and barbecue the ribs for 2 hours with the bone-side facing down.

Flip the ribs over and barbecue for another hour.

Place the ribs on a piece of foil. Mix the vinegar, beer and garlic together and pour over the ribs. Wrap into a parcel and put it back on the grill for another hour.

Unwrap the parcel, take out the ribs and put directly onto the rack for another 30 minutes, turning over halfway through. Eat with sides of your choice (see p.94).

THE TEXAS CRUTCH

The method of wrapping the meat into a little foil parcel for a part of the grilling is called the Texas Crutch and could be a tad controversial in barbecue circles. Older men especially frown at the concept but I get a consistently better result using this method. It cuts down the barbecue time, the juice that's often poured into the parcel adds flavour and it's an easy way to ensure that the meat won't dry out.

BEEF

RIBS

The cow's ribs have quite little in common with their pig counterpart. Firstly, they are much larger, but they are also tougher and contain more fat, cartilage and connective tissue. But if you cook them slow 'n' low, they will become tender, buttery and incredibly richer in flavour than pork ribs – a little bit like eating a perfectly grilled piece of rib-eye steak (with a handle).

SERVES 6

3kg/6½lb beef ribs
real Texas rub (see p.21)
hickory, oak or pecan wood smoking chips
330ml/11fl oz/1½ cups beer
foil

Since the cow is so large, there are several different varieties of ribs to choose from. The most common ones are, however, back ribs and short ribs. Back ribs come with the meat in between the bones and can usually be found at the butchers since this is what's left once the prime cuts like rib-eye steak have been taken. That might sound good but if you can choose, it's better to buy short ribs because here the meat sits on top of the bone and there's much more of it. It's also well marbled, rich in flavour and incredibly tasty to barbecue. The real cool ones choose something called dino ribs - 50cm/20in long beasts. There are also ribs that are cut sideways like Latin American asado de tira or Korean kalbi. In any case, start barbecuing beef ribs!

Prepare the ribs by trimming off any large lumps of waxy fat and pulling off the tough, paper-like silver skin on the back of the ribs. Not all ribs come with this skin, so don't panic if you can't find it. Sprinkle with the rub and leave to stand for 1 hour until it is at room temperature.

Prepare your grill for indirect cooking (see p.13). When you have a consistent temperature of somewhere between 115°C/239°F and 120°C/248°F, throw in a couple of handfuls of wood smoking chips and leave the ribs to barbecue with the bone-side facing down.

Fill a spray flask with cold beer. Spray some in your mouth and then stand prepared to spray the ribs if they start looking dry – remembering not to check too often so that the heat escapes. When the ribs have an inside temperature of about 65°C/149°F and have turned a nice dark colour, it's time to wrap them up. Cool Texans use waxed butcher paper, but if you want a juicier result, and if your guests are arriving soon, use foil, which speeds up the process.

Leave until the inside temperature is 82-87°C/179.6-188.6°F. Take the parcel out, leave to rest for 30 minutes before unwrapping it. Share the ribs out and start noshing with sides of your choice (see p.94).

A rack of beef back ribs.

My daughter Dixie is eating dino rib at Black's BBQ in Lockhart, Texas.

TEXAS
HOT LINKS

The national sausage of Texas is something in between a smoked
and a grilled banger. It should be meaty enough to be eaten
straight away, but firm enough to be broken off with
a nice snap when taking the first bite.

ABOUT 25 SAUSAGES

2 tbsp ground black pepper
2 tbsp paprika
2 tbsp chilli (chile) flakes
1 tbsp garlic powder
1½ tbsp salt
1 tsp crushed bay leaves
1 tsp whole fennel seeds
1 tsp whole mustard seeds
1 tbsp finely chopped garlic
1 tsp granulated sugar
1 beer
2kg/4½lb pork collar (neck)
1kg/2¼lb beef chuck steak
sausage casing
hickory or mesquite wood
    smoking chips

Mix all the spices, the finely chopped garlic, sugar and beer together. Dice the meat into cubes large enough to fit in your meat mincer, add the spice mixture and mix thoroughly. Leave in the fridge overnight.

About 1 hour before it's time to mince the sausage, put the meat and the mincer in the freezer – if the sausage mixture gets too hot, it will split and result in a squeaking, weird texture.

Mince the meat using the smallest grinder attachment, stir everything together again, and put back into the fridge immediately. Fry some sausage mince to taste it, if you want. Rinse the sausage casing thoroughly – at the same time, remember and forget that it's pork intestines we're talking about – and leave to soak in warm water.

Attach the sausage stuffer to the mincer, slip on the casing and tie a knot at the end. Carefully press the meat paste into the casing and continue until you have run out of either sausage mixture or casing. Twist into appropriately sized sausages and roll together. Freeze the ones you don't plan to barbecue straight away.

Prepare your grill for indirect cooking (see p.13). When you have a consistent temperature of somewhere between 110°C/230°F and 120°C/248°F, throw in a couple of handfuls of wood smoking chips, put the sausages on the rack and close the lid. Barbecue for 1–2 hours or until the inside temperature has reached 73°C/163°F. Serve with your choice of sides or hotdogueros (see p.90).

CHOPPED
BEEF
SANDWICH

It's not only pork that can be barbecued to falling-apart delicious-ness. In Central Texas, they often treat you to pulled or chopped beef too. Since beef isn't as fatty as pork, it requires that you keep an incredibly careful watch over the grill. The slightest increase in temperature and the meat will become dry, hard and boring.

SERVES 6

about 1.2kg/2¾lb well-marbled chuck steak
real Texas rub (see p.21)
hickory or mesquite wood smoking chips
hipster coffee barbecue sauce (see p.25)
aluminium roasting tray
foil

Pat the meat with the rub and leave until it is at room temperature.

Prepare your grill for indirect cooking (see p.13). When you have a consistent temperature of somewhere between 110°C/230°F and 120°C/248°F, throw in a couple of handfuls of wood smoking chips, then put the steak on the rack and close the lid. Barbecue for 2 hours.

Take the meat out, place it on an aluminium roasting tray and wrap it in foil. Put back onto the grill for more indirect cooking. Leave until the inside temperature has reached 93°C/199°F, about 3-4 hours.

Let the meat rest for 15 minutes.

Lift out of the meat juices, which you save after skimming the fat away. Pull the meat apart using two forks, removing any sinews and pour as much of the meat juice over as you need to make it moist. When it's time to eat, mix 2 tablespoons of the barbecue sauce with the meat and serve. Remember not to use too much sauce, but do leave it out in case your guests want more. Serve with cemitas (see p.102) and coleslaw of your choice (see p.116).

ANOTHER AWESOME
BEEF SANDWICH

Stuff the meat in between two slices of white sourdough bread together with some pickles, a few pickled chillies and a couple of slices of provolone or mozzarella cheese. Put it in a sandwich grill or fry in a frying pan (skillet) until the bread is crispy.

T-BONE

HOW TO NAIL THE PERFECTLY GRILLED STEAK

There's more to life than slow barbecued meat. Sometimes you're short of time, and when you are there's no shame in normal grilling. However, it doesn't mean that it's okay to start cheating with some nasty pre-marinated stuff.

SERVES 1

1 T-bone steak or other grill-friendly,
    well-marbled piece of steak
salt and freshly ground black pepper
hickory smoking wood chips

Sprinkle both sides of the meat with salt and, if you have time, leave to marinate in the fridge for 1–2 hours. You will have to wait to add pepper until serving as spices easily get charred on the outdoor grill. Take the steak out of the fridge in good time before cooking so it reaches room temperature.

Prepare your grill for two-zone grilling (see p.13). Place the meat on the side with indirect heat, the temperature should be between 110°C/230°F and 135°C/275°F. Throw in some wood smoking chips, close the lid, and barbecue until the inside temperature has reached 45°C/113°F.

Now it's time to give the meat some colour. Move to the side with direct heat (see p.13) and grill quickly over the heat until the whole surface is beautifully browned, without being burnt, and the inside temperature has reached 55–60°C/131–140°F (which means medium-rare to medium). If you want your meat well done, put this book back where you found it and defrost a fish pie instead. Enjoy together with your choice of sides (see p.94) or simply together with baked sweet potatoes (see p.122).

Part 3

EA

The further east you get in Texas, the more pork and sticky sauces you will find on the barbecue menus. Because the area stretching between Dallas in the north to Houston in the south is almost solely characterised by its proximity to the American Southern states in general – and to the Afro-American grill culture in particular.

I f East Texas and the rest of the American South states have one dish that can symbolise the darkest part of their history, it would definitely be the pork collar (neck). For this tough cut of meat full of fat and connective tissue was regarded by the slave masters as barely fit for human consumption and was thrown out to the slaves together with other 'inedible' parts like ribs and hock. The Afro-American population soon found that if you cooked these poor excuses for meat for a long time and over a low heat, the fat and collagen started to melt and after almost a whole day by the fire, you ended up with the most flavour-rich, tender, smoky, juicy piece of meat you had ever tasted – an astounding amount tastier than the boring fillet steaks the slave masters were feasting upon.

The fact is that most of East Texas' barbecue culture is born from a hard life and the necessity to survive. And it proves that necessity really is the mother of invention. The fact that the meat is almost always served pulled or chopped in these areas dates, for example, back to the times when there was no tender meat to get hold of. And the hot, sweet and sticky barbecue sauces are said to have been introduced to cover up the foul taste of meat that's gone off.

Even the word 'barbecue' came into usage due to the slave trade. When the African slaves who were first taken to the Caribbean islands later were shipped to North and South Carolina in the eighteenth century, they brought with them the Haitian Taíno people's method to grill meat and fish on a barbacot – a simple grilling rack made out of sticks. The Spanish soon Spanified the word to 'barbacoa', and when it finally started spreading in the US it became, that's right: barbecue.

Today you almost always find East Texas' best barbecue restaurants in the cities, run by Afro-Americans. These restaurants use much more pork than they do in other parts of Texas, and the sweet-sour barbecue sauces are not only regarded as a condiment but as an important component of the dish. The meat they serve is not only incredibly tasty – it's also a reminder that food, above all, is life, and that you don't always need first-class produce to create first-class dishes.

Brisket sandwich with plenty of barbecue sauce from Fargo's Pit BBQ in Bryan, Texas.

Pulled pork is slowly barbecued stringy meat with a hard cara-melised bark that holds in the juices and gives a fantastic smoky flavour. If you have only tried making pulled pork at home in the oven, you will soon discover that the authentic, barbecued variety is a completely different ball game. Since pork collar is such a forgiv-ing and pleasant cut of meat, it's also a perfect dish for the novice.

SERVES 6

about 1.2kg/2¾lb pork collar (neck) from a
    happy pig
magic dust or another paprika-based rub
    (see p.21)
hickory or apple wood smoking chips
aluminium roasting tray
200ml/7fl oz/generous ¾ cup apple juice
foil

If your pork comes with a fat cap, trim most of it off using a sharp knife. Sprinkle the meat with the rub and remember that despite the name rub you shouldn't rub it, but rather pat the spices gently into the meat. Leave to marinate in the fridge for 1–4 hours.

Prepare your grill for indirect cooking (see p.13). When you have a consistent temperature of somewhere between 110°C/230°F and 120°C/248°F, throw in a couple of handfuls of wood smoking chips, place the pork on the rack and close the lid. Barbecue until the inside temperature has reached 80°C/176°F, about 3–4 hours.

Now it's time to wrap the meat. Take the meat out of the grill and place it in an aluminium roasting tray, pour the apple juice over the meat and wrap it in foil. Leave until the inside temperature has reached 90°C/194°F, about 2–3 hours.

Leave the meat to rest for 30 minutes and then drain off the juice. Pull the meat apart using two forks, removing any bits that are too fatty and serve immediately with cemitas (see p.102), coleslaw of your choice (see p.116) and barbecue sauce of your choice (see p.24).

SMOKE ME WITH HICKORY OR APPLE WOOD.

PULLED PORK
SANDWICH

SLICED PORK SANDWICH

Sometimes you actually don't have to wait the whole day for your pulled pork to be ready. Barbecued pork collar tastes fantastic already at an inner temperature of 88°C/176°F, even if you then have to slice it, and that's just a pleasure. Put the sliced pork in a sandwich or eat together with some of my super-tasty sides.

SERVES 6

about 1.2kg/2¾lb pork collar (neck) from a happy pig
magic dust (see p.21)
hickory or apple wood smoking chips
aluminium roasting tray
200ml/7fl oz/generous ¾ cup apple juice
foil

If your pork comes with a fat cap, trim most of it off using a sharp knife. Sprinkle the meat with the rub and remember that despite the name rub you shouldn't rub it, but rather pat it gently into the meat. Leave to marinate in the fridge for 1–4 hours.

Prepare your grill for indirect cooking (see p.13). When you have a consistent temperature of somewhere between 110°C/230°F and 120°C/248°F, throw in a couple of handfuls of wood smoking chips, place the pork on the rack and close the lid. Barbecue until the inside temperature has reached 70°C/158°F.

Now it's time to wrap the meat. Take the meat out of the grill and place it in an aluminium roasting tray, pour the apple juice over the meat and wrap it in foil. Continue cooking on indirect heat until the inside temperature has reached 80°C/176°F.

Leave the meat to rest for 30 minutes and then drain off the juice. Slice thinly and serve with cemitas (see p.102), dill pickles (see p.105), pickled caramelised onion (see p.106), grated horseradish or sides of your choice (see p.94).

ON OR OFF THE BONE?

If you want to barbecue your pork like the big boys and girls, you will need to choose a whole collar weighing in at about 3-4kg/6½-8¾lb and still on the bone. A large piece will get both juicier and flashier, and the bone will act as a conductor for the heat as well as being a good indicator of when the meat is done - when the bone will easily slip out of the meat. But there are also benefits to buying smaller pieces, or even to cut a large one into smaller pieces: it will be quicker to cook it, you don't have to feed an army every time you feel like eating a pork sandwich, and, above all, you'll get more of the delicious bark.

REDNECK

PORCHETTA

The crispy, porky porchetta has to be – alongside aqueducts, road systems and gladiator games – the Italian people's greatest gift to the rest of humanity. This version is made from pork belly and ditches the lame herbs in favour of pure smoky yumminess.

SERVES 10

1 whole (about 2kg/4½lb) pork belly (side)

Texas rub (see p.21)

salt

kitchen string

apple wood smoking chips

Cut the rind off your pork belly using a sharp knife. Trim some of the fat off the rind. Pat the meat with the rub and roll together with the smooth side facing out. Leave to marinate in the fridge while you are fixing with the rind.

Preheat the oven to 175°C/347°F/Gas mark 3. Put the rind face down in an ovenproof dish. Pour in enough water until the rind is covered, and place in the oven for about 1 hour until the rind has softened. Take the rind out of the dish, leave to dry and cool, and then score the rind leaving about 1cm/½in gap between each cut. Rub with a generous amount of salt.

Wrap the rind around the meat. If it's too big, cut it so that it fits perfectly and doesn't wrap around itself. If the rind has shrunk in the oven, leave the bottom side of the meat uncovered. Tie up nicely with kitchen string.

Prepare your grill for indirect cooking (see p.13). Make sure to give it a good blazing, as the grill needs to come up to a temperature of 220-225°C/425-437°F to get the pork rind crackling nicely - if it doesn't work, put the porchetta in the oven instead. Grill for 30 minutes then turn down the heat (or if you've used the oven: transfer it over to the grill). When the temperature is around 140°C/284°F, throw in a couple of handfuls of wood smoking chips and close the lid. Barbecue until the inside temperature has reached 70°C/158°F, about 3-4 hours.

Let the meat rest for 30 minutes without wrapping it in foil - or the crackling will go soft. Slice it nice and thin using a sharp carving knife. Serve with white sourdough bread (see p.98), maple mustard barbecue sauce (see p.25), sliced apple fried in butter or sides of your choice (see p.94).

OTHER WAYS TO SERVE BARBECUED PORCHETTA

BARBECUE PORK REUBEN

Serve porchetta on a slice of toasted sourdough with sauerkraut, home-made Thousand Island dressing and melted Emmental cheese.

BARBECUE PORK CUBAN SANDWICH

Put thinly sliced porchetta, provolone or mozzarella cheese, sliced dill pickles and mustard in a sourdough baguette and toast in a sandwich grill or a frying pan (skillet).

BARBECUE PORK GRILLED CHEESE

Put Emmental cheese and porchetta between two slices of sourdough. Toast in a sandwich grill or a frying pan (skillet).

BABY

BACK RIBS

RECIPE OVERLEAF

Baby back ribs, or just back ribs, are shorter, curvier and often meatier than the larger, straighter spare rib. They are also practically packed in portion size by Mother Nature – a whole rack, plus sides, is normally perfect as a main for a hungry person.

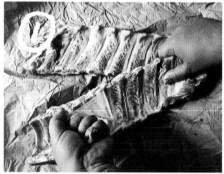

SERVES 6

6 whole racks (about 2-3kg/4½-
    6½lb) of baby back ribs
magic dust or other paprika-
    based rub (see p.21)
hickory or apple wood smoking
    chips
foil

200ml/7fl oz/generous ¾ cup
    apple juice
barbecue sauce of your choice
    (see p.24)

Prepare the ribs by removing the tough, paper-like silver skin from the back of the ribs. Sprinkle with the rub and remember that despite the name rub, you shouldn't rub it in but rather pat it in gently. Leave to marinate in the fridge for 1–4 hours.

Prepare your grill for indirect cooking (see p.13). When you have a consistent temperature of somewhere between 110°C/230°F and 120°C/248°F, throw in a couple of handfuls of wood smoking chips and leave the ribs to barbecue for 2 hours with the bone-side facing down.

Flip the ribs over and barbecue for another 30 minutes.

Place the ribs on top of a piece of foil. Pour over the apple juice and wrap it up into a parcel. Put back on the grill for another hour.

Take the ribs out of the parcel, brush with barbecue sauce and put directly on the grill rack for 15 minutes to caramelise the sauce, flipping over halfway through. Serve whole to your happy guests with your choice of sides (see p.94).

HOW TO TEST IF YOUR RIBS ARE COOKED

Less thoughtful grill restaurants normally boil their ribs to get that perfect falling-off-the-bone texture. The problem with this is that all the flavour disappears into the water plus that really good ribs shouldn't even fall off the bone. The perfect texture should instead be so tender that if you take a bite you shouldn't have to tear off the meat with your teeth, but at the same time all the meat shouldn't fall off the bone either. Instead, a beautiful, tooth-shaped crescent should appear.

1. PORK LOIN/
BABY BACK RIBS

2. RIBS

OINK!

ST LOUIS-STYLE SPARE RIBS

Spare ribs are an ingenious invention (perfect tender meat on a stick!) but with a major design fault: that lump of fat, cartilage and connective tissue at the end of the rib. Luckily, you can trim off the rubbish yourself, St Louis-style.

SERVES 6

4 whole racks (about 3kg/6½lb) of pork spare ribs
magic dust or other paprika-based rub (see p.21)
hickory or apple wood smoking chips

foil
200ml/7fl oz/generous ¾ cup apple juice
barbecue sauce of your choice (see p.24)

Prepare your ribs according to the chart on the right. Sprinkle with the rub and leave to marinate in the fridge for 1–4 hours.

Prepare your grill for indirect cooking (see p.13). When you have a consistent temperature of somewhere between 110°C/230°F and 120°C/248°F, throw in a couple of handfuls of wood smoking chips and leave the ribs to barbecue for 2 hours with the bone-side facing down.

Flip the ribs over and barbecue for another hour.

Place the ribs on top of a piece of foil. Pour over the apple juice and wrap it up into a parcel. Put back on the grill for another hour.

Take the ribs out of the parcel, brush with barbecue sauce and put directly on the grill rack for 15 minutes to caramelise the sauce, flipping over halfway through. Cut them between the bones and let the gnashing commence. Serve with a choice of sides (see p.94).

OINK!

TRIM THE RIBS

In contrast to the small baby back ribs, the larger spare ribs contain a lot of unnecessary cartilage and fat that doesn't taste nice.

You can, however, rectify this by trimming them St Louis-style – that is, cutting off the top cartilage bit attached to the ribs, so you end up with a nice square shape and completely straight ribs.

At the back of the bones, there is also a thin silver skin that becomes tough and paper-like if you cook it. Don't forget to remove this. Just carefully insert a finger in between the meat and the membrane and then pull.

Voilà! Now your previously messy ribs are both nice and neat and will be record-breakingly tender after barbecuing. Just pour over the rub and chuck them on the grill.

RIB SANDWICH

If you, against all suppositions, end up with leftovers from your spare ribs at some point, you'll just have to make a rib sandwich the next day. Apart from a sandwich made out of solid gold, it's the most luxurious sandwich you can ever munch down.

SERVES 1

meat from spare ribs or baby
   back ribs (as much as you can
   scrape off and that will fit in a
   sandwich)
barbecue sauce of your choice
   (see p.24)
pickled caramelised onions
   (see p.106)
a few slices Emmental cheese
1 handful of rocket (arugula)
sourdough baguette or sourdough white bread (see p.98)

Using a knife, scrape off
as much meat from the ribs
as you possibly can.

Heat the meat in a frying pan
(skillet). If you have some leftover
barbecue sauce, you can drizzle
it over the meat now.

Put the meat, onions,
cheese and rocket in a
sourdough baguette or in
between slices of sourdough
and toast in a sandwich
grill or a frying pan.

SMOKY
CHICKEN
WINGS

To smoke your own chicken wings produces an almost incomprehensibly tastier result than the newly defrosted buffalo wings you can get from your local restaurant. They're smoky, hot, juicy and not particularly difficult at all to do – at least not if you know how. Best eaten while executing a hobby.

SERVES 6

18 chicken wings
   (about 1.2kg/2¾lb)
½ tbsp salt
red rub (see p.21)
½ lemon
½ orange
mesquite wood smoking chips
Carolina hot 'n' nasty (see p.26)

If you're not careful, the chicken skin can get tough and rubbery when barbecued. To prevent this, prepare the chicken by salting the skin slightly and leave to dry uncovered in the fridge for about 4 hours. When it's time to barbecue, pat the chicken with kitchen paper to remove the moisture and salt. Cut the wing tip off at the joint and pat the rub into the meat. Grate over lemon and orange zest.

Prepare your grill for indirect cooking (see p.13) and make sure it keeps a steady temperature of around 120°C/248°F. Throw in a couple of handfuls of wood smoking chips and smoke the wings for 2 hours.

Take the chicken out of the grill and get ready for direct cooking. Brush with barbecue sauce and grill directly above the charcoal until the skin is crispy and the sauce is caramelised. Serve with Tabasco or other chilli sauce, celery stalks and beer.

SERVES 6

WAFFLES
4 eggs, separated
50g/2oz/4 tbsp melted butter,
    chilled
100ml/3½fl oz/scant ½ cup milk
200g/7oz/scant 11½ cups plain
    (all-purpose) flour
2 tsp baking powder
½ tsp salt
2 tsp finely chopped fresh
    rosemary

Chicken
100g/3½oz/⅓ cup salt
330ml/11fl oz/1½ cups beer
1 whole (about 1.2kg/2¾lb)
    chicken
red rub (see p.21)
mesquite wood smoking chips
maple mustard barbecue sauce
    (see p.26)

For the chicken, stir the salt and beer together until the salt
has dissolved. Cut the chicken along the spine and open it out.
Rinse the chicken and leave to marinate in the beer brine in the
fridge overnight, preferably with a weight on top.

If you don't watch out, chicken skin can get tough and
rubbery when you barbecue it. To prevent this, take the chicken
out of the brine in good time before cooking and leave it to dry
uncovered in the fridge for about 4 hours. When it's time to
grill, pat in the rub.

Prepare your grill for indirect cooking (see p.13) and make
sure it keeps a steady temperature of around 115°C/239°F.
Throw in a couple of handfuls of wood smoking chips and
barbecue the chicken with the bone-side facing down for about
3 hours or until the inside temperature has reached 73°C/163°F.

Take the chicken out of the grill and get ready for direct
cooking (see p.13). Brush the chicken sparingly with the barbecue
sauce, and grill with the skin side facing down directly over the
charcoals for a couple of minutes or until the skin is crispy.

Whisk the egg yolks in a bowl until fluffy then carefully stir in
the chilled melted butter and milk. Mix the flour, baking powder, salt
and rosemary together in another bowl and fold into the batter.
Whisk the egg whites in a separate bowl until you can turn the
bowl upside down above your head without going all eggy. Fold
the egg whites into the batter and bake the waffles.

Assemble the sandwich by placing two rashers of crispy
bacon on top of a newly baked rosemary waffle, then some
barbecued chicken, and to finish off, some extra maple mustard
barbecue sauce and perhaps also a second waffle on top.

CHICKEN & WAFFLE

SANDWICH

Part 4

WEST

TEXAS

The barbecue in West Texas is somewhat different in comparison to that of the rest of the state. Here the food is distinguished by Mexican flavours but also the cooking methods are different. Inspired by the barbacoa, a technique called smoke braising is often used: first, you smoke the meat and then you leave it to slowly braise wrapped in either foil or banana leaves.

I f you ask someone to close their eyes and think about Texas, it's probably the enormous sparsely populated desert between West Texas and North Mexico that they see before their eyes. It's here, in what's called 'the most remote place in America', that you'll find all those things associated with the American West: cactus, ranches, long-horned cows, rattle snakes and rusty old pick-ups with a rifle showing in the rear window.

'If this is God's own country', the journalist A.A. Gill wrote during one of his visits, 'then God moved out some time ago, taking everything of interest with him'. But like anywhere else in the state, West Texas isn't quite as desolate, conservative and boring as you might think at first sight. Especially the area around the Big Bend national park is, on the contrary, a place 'where the misfits fit in'. Because ever since the minimalist artist Donald Judd moved to the small town of Marfa in the

1970s, the desolated area has slowly but surely become populated by artists, foodies, off-gridders, hippies and New York fashion photographers undergoing a life crisis, and today it's a strange mix between the hip Brooklyn neighbourhood Williamsburg and the proper wild west. Nowadays it's also a popular place for shooting Hollywood productions, and movies like *No Country for Old Men* and *There Will Be Blood* have been filmed in the area. West Texas is simply, like the magazine *Vanity Fair* described it, a place 'where you can do doughnuts in the middle of town in your jeep and then go and drink a $200 (£120) bottle of Barolo'.

In this area, the local cuisine is almost exclusively characterised by the proximity to Mexico and at the same time, the many ranches that supply the produce. And it's the Mexicans who've been working on these ranches since the nineteenth century who contribute with the cooking methods. This is because they were often given less desirable meat cuts like skirt steaks and cow and sheep's heads as a part of their salary. The thin bits of meat were grilled quickly over an open mesquite fire and were sliced to be used for fajitas, while the cows' heads were wrapped in banana leaves, just like at home in Mexico, and were buried in the ground and covered with charcoal until the meat was tender and fell off the bone. This meat was perfect for using in tacos together with a salsa hotter than the sun and some coriander.

The chef, artist and musician Adam Bork is peaking out of his world-famous food truck Food Shark in Marfa, Texas.

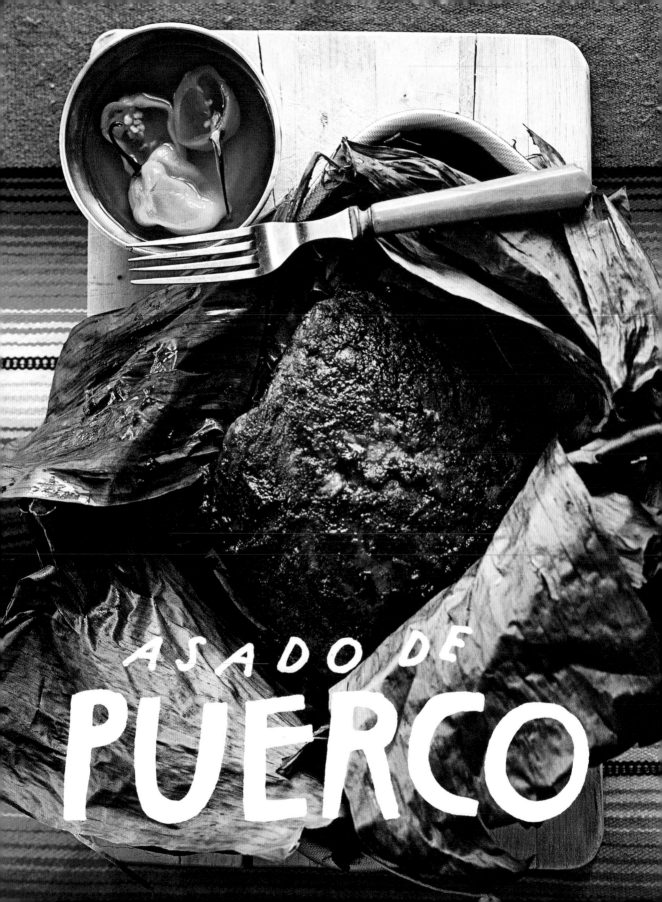

ASADO DE PUERCO

This Mexican pulled-pork variety tastes hot from ancho chilli, sour from vinegar and heavenly from basking in the heat from the grill the whole day. Banana leaves are often stocked in Asian food stores so don't ditch them. They give flavour and look pretty cool to unwrap in front of your stunned guests at the dining table.

SERVES 6

about 1.2kg/2¾ lb pork collar (neck) from a happy pig
Texas rub (see p.21)
hickory or apple wood smoking chips
5 dried chillies, eg ancho
50ml/2fl oz/scant ¼ cup distilled vinegar (12%)
2 garlic cloves
3 tbsp granulated sugar
½ tsp salt
½ tsp ground cumin
¼ tsp dried oregano
banana leaves
200ml/7fl oz/generous ¾ cup pineapple juice
kitchen string

Pat the meat with the rub. Prepare your grill for indirect cooking (see p.13). When you have a consistent temperature of somewhere between 110°C/230°F and 120°C/248°F, throw in a couple of handfuls of wood smoking chips and barbecue the meat for 2 hours.

Make the adobo (the sauce) by toasting the dried chillies in a dry frying pan (skillet) until they start smelling divine. Put them into a bowl, cover with water and leave for 30 minutes. Drain the chillies, then remove the stalks and deseed, then mix with the vinegar, 100ml/3½fl oz/scant ½ cup water, the garlic, sugar, salt, cumin and oregano in a blender until you have a red paste.

Place the pork on a couple of banana leaves in an ovenproof dish, pour over the adobo paste, then the pineapple juice, and wrap up properly using more leaves. Tie with kitchen string if needed. Don't worry if some pineapple juice drips out into the dish, it will still help to braise the meat.

Barbecue until the inside temperature has reached 90°C/194°F, about 3½ hours.

Leave the meat to rest for 10 minutes. Open the parcel in front of your astounded dinner guests and pull the meat apart coarsely using two forks, removing any pieces that are too fatty, and serve immediately with sourdough tortillas (see p.100), pickled red onions (see p.106), Carolina hot 'n' nasty (see p.26), pickles of your choice (see p.104), chopped fresh coriander (cilantro) and white onion.

HOW TO MAKE COCHINITA PIBIL

If you want to make the classic Mexican pork dish cochinita pibil, which can be traced back to the Mayans, follow the instructions above but instead of an adobo, make a spice mix using the following ingredients: 5 tbsp achiote seeds (also called annatto and can be found in specialist grocery stores), 1½ tbsp dried oregano, 1½ tbsp ground black pepper, 1 tsp ground cumin, ½ tsp cloves, 1 tsp ground cinnamon, 15 garlic cloves, 200ml/7fl oz freshly squeezed lime juice and 100ml/3½fl oz orange juice. Blend. Rub. Barbecue.

The traditional Mexican barbacoa was in its original form a simple grilling hole in the ground where a pot filled with vegetables would be placed under the meat to collect all the tasty meat juices. That way you got, with the minimal amount of effort, a smoky and luxuriously brothy soup for starter *and* a perfectly barbecued bit of meat to fill your main course tacos with.

SERVES 6–8

Texas rub (see p.21)
about 3kg/6½ lb lamb steak on the bone
apple wood smoking chips
2 dried chillies, eg ancho
2 dried chipotle chillies
400g/14oz canned tomatoes
4 garlic cloves, crushed
2 potatoes, diced
1 brown onion, diced
2 carrots, diced
2 celery stalks, diced
1 fresh rosemary sprig (or ½ tsp dried)
400g/14oz canned black beans
salt and freshly ground black pepper
oil, for deep-frying
4–6 thin corn tortillas
2 avocados, peeled, stoned and diced
finely chopped fresh coriander (cilantro)

Pat the rub into the lamb and leave to marinate in the fridge for 2 hours.

Prepare your grill for indirect cooking (see p.13). When you have a consistent temperature of somewhere between 110°C/230°F and 120°C/248°F, throw in a couple of handfuls of wood smoking chips and leave the lamb to barbecue for 2 hours with the fat cap facing up.

Remove the stalks and deseed the dried chillies, then boil in a small pan of water for about 15 minutes. Blend to a smooth paste.

When the meat has barbecued for 2 hours, transfer it to a casserole dish – alternatively, an aluminium roasting tray – and add the tomatoes, 200ml/7fl oz/ generous ¾ cup water, the blended chilli paste, crushed garlic, diced potatoes, onion, carrot and celery. Add a sprig of rosemary, salt and pepper, and cover with a lid or wrap it in foil.

Braise slowly on the grill for 2–4 hours until the inside temperature is around 87°C/188.6°F. Alternatively, cook in an oven preheated to 120°C/250°F/Gas mark ½ . Take out the meat, wrap it in foil and leave to rest while you skim off the fat from the braising juices and add the beans, which just need to warm through. Season to taste with salt and pepper.

Heat the oil for deep-frying to 180°C/350°F. Cut the corn tortillas into strips and deep-fry in the oil until crispy. Leave to drain on kitchen paper.

Serve by ladling the bean soup into bowls and let your guests choose how much diced avocado, chopped coriander (cilantro) and tortilla crisps they want to garnish with.

When taco time is drawing near, just unwrap the parcel and take out the steak, shred the tender and fallingapart meat with a couple of forks and serve with sourdough tortillas (see p.100), grilled tomato salsa (see p.114) and finely chopped white onion.

BARBACOA
DE BORREGO

BEEF BARBACOA

In Mexico, real barbacoa is made from the whole head of a cow that's been wrapped in banana leaves and buried in the ground together with some burning charcoal. However, due to practical reasons, in this recipe I have chosen to replace the head with braising steak. Perhaps not as spectacular but easier to source and doesn't scare the kids.

SERVES 6–8

Texas rub (see p.21)
1–2kg/2¼–4½lb braising steak
hickory wood smoking chips
2 dried chillies, eg ancho
2 dried chipotle chillies
330ml/11fl oz/1½ cups beer
1 tbsp chilli powder
1 tsp ground cumin
1 tsp dried coriander seeds
2 tsp dried oregano
2–3 tbsp plain (all-purpose) flour
6 garlic cloves, finely chopped
2 brown onions, sliced
1–2 fresh chillies, sliced
salt and freshly ground black pepper

Pat the rub into the meat and leave to marinate in the fridge for 2 hours.

Prepare your grill for indirect cooking (see p.13). When you have a consistent temperature of somewhere between 110°C/230°F and 120°C/248°F, throw in a couple of handfuls of wood smoking chips and barbecue the steak for 2 hours.

Meanwhile, remove the stalks and deseed the dried chillies, then boil them in a dash of water for about 15 minutes. Blend to a smooth paste.

Once the meat is done, place it in a casserole dish - alternatively, in an aluminium roasting tray - and pour over the beer, chilli paste, spices, flour, garlic, onion and chilli. Season with salt and pepper, and cover with a lid or wrap it in foil.

Braise slowly in the grill at 120°C/248°F for 2–4 hours until the inside temperature has reached about 90°C/194°F. Alternatively, cook in an oven preheated to 120°C/250°F/Gas mark ½. Leave to rest for 15 minutes, then divide the juicy and falling-apart meat using two forks into the braising juices and serve with sourdough tortillas (see p.100), crème fraîche, smoky tomato salsa (see p.114), lime wedges, finely chopped fresh coriander (cilantro) and white onion.

ANCHO BRAISED

SHORT RIBS

SERVES 6

real Texas rub (see p.21)
about 3kg/6½ lb beef short ribs
mesquite or pecan wood smoking chips
½ brown onion, chopped
2-4 fresh chillies, eg medium-hot chillies
    or jalapeño, finely chopped
3 garlic cloves, chopped
rapeseed (canola) oil, for frying
4 dried chillies, eg ancho
330ml/11fl oz/1½ cups Dr Pepper, not diet
salt
aluminium roasting tray
foil

Pat the rub into the meat and marinate for 1 hour at room temperature.

Prepare your grill for indirect cooking (see p.13). When you have a consistent temperature of somewhere between 110°C/230°F and 120°C/248°F, throw in a couple of handfuls of wood smoking chips and leave the ribs to barbecue for 2 hours bone-side down.

Sauté the onion, chillies and garlic in oil until soft. Remove the stalks and deseed the dried chillies, then add to the pan with the Dr Pepper and simmer for about 10 minutes.

Blend to a smooth braising juice and season to taste with salt.

Place the ribs in an aluminium roasting tray, pour over the braising juice, wrap it in foil, and continue barbecuing until the inside temperature is around 82-97°C/179.6-206.6°F, about 2 hours.

Take the ribs out of the parcel, leave to rest for 5 minutes, and eat straight off the bones or tear the meat off using two forks. Pour over some braising juice and eat in a sourdough tortilla (see p.100) with salsa of your choice (see p.114), finely chopped fresh coriander (cilantro) and white onion.

CAN I REPLACE SHORT RIBS?

Beef short ribs can sometimes be a bit tricky to source (find out more in my little buying guide on p.42). So if you can't get hold of them, or just feel like eating pork, this recipe also works for baby back ribs. Prepare in pretty much the same way, but stop cooking when the inside temperature has reached about 90°C/194°F (or when they seem nice and tender).

CHICKEN MOLE

The complex, flavourful mole sauce is the national dish of Mexico and is traditionally served with rice and poached chicken – but like everything else, it will be tastier if you barbecue it and serve it as a taco. If you want to be fancy, throw a mole party with chicken on the barbecue and a pan of mole sauce bubbling away over an open fire – very cosy!

SERVES 4

1 barbecued chicken, preferably pollo de asado (see p.86)

MOLE
50ml/2fl oz/scant ½ cup rapeseed oil
5 dried chillies, eg ancho, deseeded
5 dried guajillo chillies, or whatever you can find
500ml/18fl oz/generous 2 cups chicken stock
2 tbsp almonds
2 tbsp sesame seeds
2 tbsp salted peanuts
2 tbsp pecan nuts
2 tbsp pumpkin seeds
200g/7oz plum tomatoes
200g/7oz tomatillos or physalis (Cape gooseberries)
1 brown onion
8 garlic cloves
1 plantain
1 tbsp rapeseed oil, for frying
100g/3½oz/scant ⅔ cup raisins
4 cloves
½ star anise
3cm/1¼in cinnamon stick
3 whole allspice berries
1 tbsp ground black pepper
1 tsp dried oregano
1 tsp salt
1 slice bread, toasted
30g/1oz dark chocolate, broken into pieces
50g/2oz/¼ cup brown sugar
2 tbsp sesame seeds

Heat the oil in a pan and throw in the deseeded dried chillies for a quick 30-second toasting. Make sure they don't start to smoke or the mole will be bitter. Transfer to a saucepan, pour over some of the stock and leave to simmer for 30 minutes. Purée the chilli with the stock and pass through a sieve back into the oil you toasted them in. Leave to simmer until it starts to thicken.

Toast the almonds, sesame seeds, peanuts, pecan nuts and pumpkin seeds in a dry non-stick pan. Blend to a fine powder then add to the chilli together with the rest of the chicken stock. Roast the tomatoes, tomatillos, onion and garlic whole in the oven until almost burned. Blend and stir into the chilli mixture. Slice the plantain, fry in some oil until soft, then blend together with the raisins and add to the sauce. Toast the spices in a dry pan, blitz to a fine powder in a blender, and add to the sauce. Lastly, blend the toasted bread together with chocolate and sugar and add to the sauce.

Leave to simmer for about 2 hours. Barbecue the chicken according to the instructions on p.86. Pour over some mole and sprinkle the sesame seeds over the chicken during the final 10 minutes of cooking. Serve with sourdough tortillas (see p.100), chopped coriander (cilantro) and white onion.

POLLO DE ASADO

Pollo de asado is a kind of mesquite barbecued chicken from the northern parts of Mexico and has become one of the absolute standard taco truck dishes all over Texas. And once you have tried it, it's easy to understand why: it's smoky, crispy and hot.

SERVES 4

100ml/3½fl oz/1/3 cup salt
330ml/11fl oz/1½ cups beer
3 tbsp Tabasco or other chilli sauce
1 whole (about 1.2kg/2¾lb) chicken
red rub (see p.21)
mesquite wood smoking chips

Mix the salt, beer and Tabasco sauce together using a fork until the salt has dissolved into some kind of turbo-fuelled brine. Cut the chicken along the spine and open it out. Rinse the chicken and leave to chill in the brine overnight, preferably with a weight on top.

If you don't watch out, the chicken skin can get tough and rubbery when you barbecue it, so to prevent this take the chicken out of the brine in good time before cooking and leave it to dry uncovered in the fridge for about 4 hours. When it's time to grill, pat in the rub.

Prepare your grill for indirect cooking (see p.13) and make sure it keeps a steady temperature of around 115°C/239°F.

Throw in a couple of handfuls of wood smoking chips and barbecue the chicken with the bone-side facing down for about 3 hours, or until the inside temperature has reached 73°C/163°F.

Remove the chicken from the grill and get ready for direct cooking (see p.13). Grill with the skin-side facing down directly over the charcoals for a couple of minutes or until the skin is crispy. Cut the chicken into strips and serve as tacos with sourdough tortillas (see p.100), smoky tomato salsa (see p.114), finely chopped coriander (cilantro) and white onion.

IF YOU'RE LOOKIN' YOU AIN'T COOKIN'

SAUERKRAUT HOTDOGUERO

AVOCADO SALSA HOTDOGUERO

MAPLE BACON HOT DOGUERO

COLESLAW HOTDOGUERO

RECIPE OVERLEAF

HOTDOGUEROS

In various places in south-west America, you can find hotdogueros – sausage men who serve the kind of hot dog that you will find in the Mexican state Sonora. Here are some variations.

SAUERKRAUT HOTDOGUERO

1 Texas hot link (see p.44)
1 hot dog bun (see p.102)
sauerkraut
dill pickles (see p.105)

Barbecue the sausage (see p.44). Put it in the bun and spoon some sauerkraut on to one side of the sausage and dill pickles on the other. Then try to fit everything in your mouth in one go. It just **has** to work.

AVOCADO SALSA HOTDOGUERO

1 Texas hot link (see p.44)
1 hot dog bun (see p.102)
½ avocado
½ fresh green chilli, eg medium-hot chilli or jalapeño
fresh coriander (cilantro), to taste
½ white onion
1 lime wedge
feta cheese

Barbecue the sausage (see p.44). Put it in the bun. Finely chop the avocado, chilli, coriander (cilantro) and onion, and spoon over the top. Squeeze over the lime and crumble some feta cheese on top.

MAPLE BACON HOTDOGUERO

1 Texas hot link (see p.44)
1 hot dog bun (see p.102)
2 bacon rashers (slices)
1 tbsp maple syrup
3-4 super-crispy onion rings (see p.118)

Barbecue the sausage (see p.44). Put it in the bun. On each side of the sausage stuff crispy fried bacon slices that you have brushed with some maple syrup. Finish off by putting some onion rings on top of the sausage. Ingenious.

COLESLAW HOTDOGUERO

1 Texas hot link (see p.44)
1 beetroot
oil, for deep-frying
1 hot dog bun (see p.102)
3 tbsp classic coleslaw (see p.117)
barbecue sauce of your choice (see p.24)

Barbecue the sausage (see p.44). Slice fresh beetroot into super-thin slices. Heat the oil for deep-frying to 180°C/350°F, and deep-fry the beetroot until crispy. Leave to drain on kitchen paper. Put the sausage in the bun. Spoon over some coleslaw and add a couple of beetroot crisps. Drizzle over barbecue sauce.

SONORAN HOTDOGUERO

2 bacon rashers (slices)
1 Texas hot link (see p.44)
1 hot dog bun (see p.102)
1 slice Cheddar
½ tomato
½ avocado
finely chopped fresh coriander (cilantro) and white onion
50g/2oz/scant ¼ cup mayonnaise
2 tsp green Tabasco or other chilli sauce

Wrap the bacon around the sausage and barbecue (see p.44). Line the bun with a slice of cheese and add the sausage. Stuff thin slices of tomato and avocado next to the sausage, sprinkle over some chopped coriander (cilantro) and onion and, finally, drizzle over the mayonnaise that you have mixed with chilli sauce. Serve to someone who has proved themselves worthy, with shoestring fries (see p.122).

SONORAN HOTDOGUERO

FAJITAS

Skirt fajitas might not be genuine barbecue. But it's a classic Tejano dish, which in its original form is so delicious, and easy, that it just has to be included in this book. Fajita means 'little belt' and refers to the skirt steak that is traditionally used. If you can't find one, go to a butcher's that sells South American meat – or replace with flank steak.

SERVES 4

1 skirt steak or flank steak (about 1kg/2¼lb)
2 red onions
4 fresh chillies, eg medium-hot chillies or jalapeño
4 pointed peppers
mesquite wood smoking chips

MARINADE
2 limes
400ml/14fl oz/1¾ cups pineapple juice
200ml/7fl oz/generous ¾ cup Japanese soy sauce
4 garlic cloves, crushed

For the marinade, grate the lime zest, squeeze out the juice and mix with the pineapple juice, soy sauce and crushed garlic. Place the meat in a plastic bag together with the marinade and leave in the fridge overnight.

Prepare the grill for cooking with direct heat. Grill thick slices of onion until they start to soften and nice grill stripes appear. Put the chilli and pointed pepper on the grill and leave until the skins have blackened, then place in a plastic bag and leave until the skins fall off. Deseed and slice into nice stripes.

Leave the meat until it is at room temperature then pat dry with kitchen paper (paper towels). Grill quickly and as hot as ol' Betty can manage until the meat seems medium rare, or the inside temperature has reached 57°C/134.6°F. Leave to rest for a couple of minutes and slice thinly against the meat's fibres. Serve in a sourdough tortilla (see p.100) with the grilled onion, pointed peppers and chillies.

PERFECT FAJITAS USING YOUR CHIMNEY STARTER

Doesn't your grill get hot enough to quickly cook such a thin cut of meat like skirt steak? Try the grill guru Meathead's chimney starter method. Put charcoal in the starter and place it onto the grill, put a grilling rack on top and cook quickly on the intensive jet stream of heat that comes off it.

Part 5

STI

Perhaps you're feeling like growing your own sourdough starter but are worried that you'd get sourdough bullied on Facebook? Then keep this in mind: cowboys used sourdough every day and how much did they care about what anyone else thought? That's right, not a damn. So follow this guide and you can bake wonderful cowboy sourdough bread in a matter of days.

DAY 1
Whisk 500ml/18fl oz/generous 2 cups lukewarm water and 500g/1lb 2oz/3½ cups plain (all-purpose) flour (preferably biodynamic as it's easier to get started) together in a large bowl. Pour the mixture into a clean glass jar and tie a piece of fabric over the top. If it's around 20-25°C/68-77°F outside, place the jar in the sun so that natural spores can kick-start the fermentation process (hopefully). If it's cold, put it somewhere warm in the kitchen. If the jar is outside: take it inside in the evenings or if it gets cold or starts to rain.

DAY 2
Today you don't have to do much. If it has started to bubble: congratulations, a sourdough is coming along. If there's a layer of liquid on the top: stir it down. If this liquid is red or green: throw it away and start again.

DAY 3
Do like day 2. If it has started to bubble, it's done. In which case, feed the sourdough with 200g/7oz/scant 1½ cups plain (all-purpose) flour, and some lukewarm water if it gets too thick. The consistency should be like pancake batter. Leave to stand for 6 hours, then put a lid on top and put it into the fridge. If nothing's happened, wait for another day.

DAY 4
No bubbles? Throw away and start afresh.

BAKING WITH THE SOURDOUGH
Use as much as needed for the recipe.

FEEDING THE SOURDOUGH
About once a week, you will need to feed the sourdough so it doesn't die. If it does, just throw it away, or use about 200g/7oz of the sourdough, then stir in 100ml/3½fl oz/scant ½ cup lukewarm water and 100g/3½oz/¾ cup plain (all-purpose) flour and leave the jar to stand at room temperature for about 6 hours before putting it back in the fridge.

SOURDOUGH
WHITE BREAD

Now I'm not going to lie: I actually think those mass-produced tin loaves filled to the brim with additives that accompany every barbecue meal in Texas are quite nice. However, this particular sourdough loaf is actually even tastier. The recipe is also, thanks to the sourdough master Martin Johansson's genial fold-and-rest method, incredibly easy.

1 LOAF

about 200g/7oz wheat sourdough
400g/14oz/scant 2½ cups strong white
  bread flour, plus extra for dusting
½ tsp salt
butter or oil, for greasing

Put the sourdough, 250ml/9fl oz/generous 1 cup water, the flour and salt into a bowl and mix into a dough. Cover with a tea towel and leave to rest for 45 minutes.

Fold the dough in the bowl a few times by pulling gently in the edges of the dough and folding in towards the middle. Leave to rest for 30 minutes.

Repeat the folding and leave to rest for 30 minutes. Fold one last time and leave to rest for 1 hour.

Take the dough out of the bowl and place on a floured work surface. Fold the edges of the dough towards the middle to get a tight surface on the dough. Leave to rest on the work surface for 30 minutes.

Form into a loaf shape and place into a greased oblong loaf tin.

Leave to rise for 3-4 hours at room temperature. Preheat the oven to 250°C/482°F/ Gas mark 9 and bake the sourdough for 30 minutes. If needed, reduce the oven temperature to 200°C/400°F/Gas mark 6 halfway through if the bread has turned a nice colour by then.

SOURDOUGH TORTILLAS

Before tortillas became tortillas they were called pan de campo and were made from sourdough baked over an open fire out on the prairie. These sourdough tortillas are inspired by the prairie and are richer in flavour and offer a bit more bite than the standard wheat tortilla. For extra-festive occasions, use the maximum butter (MB) method (see below).

12 LARGE OR 24 SMALL TORTILLAS

150g/5oz wheat sourdough
700g/1½ lb/5 cups plain (all-purpose) flour, plus extra
    for dusting
1½ tsp salt
100g/3½ oz/scant ½ cup melted butter

Put all the ingredients into a bowl, add 250ml/9fl oz/generous 1 cup hot water and mix into a dough. Knead the dough for about 10 minutes. Cover with a tea towel and leave to rest for 1 hour.

Divide the dough into 12 or 24 portions and put on a floured work surface. Mould into small balls. The rounder the dough ball, the rounder the tortilla. Roll out the dough as thinly as humanly possible, about 1mm/1/32in. You should almost be able to see the work surface through it.

Fry the tortilla in a dry non-stick pan, not too hot and not for too long. Or it will go crispy instead. As a guide, when the small brown bubbles appear after about 20-30 seconds in a pan, it's time to flip it over.

Since a tortilla should be soft and smooth, you will need to make use of the condensation that appears to soften the bread after baking it. So put them in a plastic bag or a tortilla warmer directly after frying and wait for a minute until soft. A spray bottle with some water may also come in handy.

THE MB METHOD
(MAXIMUM BUTTER METHOD)

Take 100g/3½oz/scant ½ cup butter out of the fridge and leave until it is at room temperature. Follow the instructions for sourdough tortillas up until cooking them, at which point spread them with butter instead of frying them.

When all the dough tortillas are buttered, roll them up into small cigar shapes then roll out to double their length.

Roll up these dough snakes so they look like little cinnamon swirls. Press down to flatten them out a little and dust with flour if needed.

Now it's time to roll out the cinnamon swirl to a tortilla. Continue from rolling them out in the recipe to the left.

CEMITAS

These Mexican buns can be used just as well for hamburgers and pulled pork as for your breakfast bap and hotdogueros – in which case, just mould them into hot dog bun shapes instead of round buns.

MAKES 12–14 BUNS

1.1kg/2½lb/scant 8 cups plain (all-purpose) flour, plus extra for dusting
2 tsp salt
2 tbsp granulated sugar
2 tsp dried yeast
5 eggs
100g/3½oz/scant ½ cup melted butter, cooled
300ml/10fl oz/1¼ cups cultured buttermilk
sesame seeds, for sprinkling

Mix all the dry ingredients together in a bowl. Whisk 4 eggs and the melted cooled butter together in another bowl. Heat the buttermilk very carefully; it should be about body temperature but without starting to split (preferably).

Mix everything together and knead into a dough. As it's still quite sticky, the easiest thing to do is to run it in a food processor for 10-15 minutes or use electric dough hooks. Cover and leave to rise for 1½ hours.

Divide the dough into 12 portions. If you want to make round burger buns, roll a portion of dough in some flour, place in your cupped hand and grab the edges and fold towards the middle until a beautiful, tight bun shape appears. Place the bun on a baking tray and flatten out slightly with your hand. If you want to make hot dog buns, divide the dough into 14 portions and roll out to oblong buns, about 12 x 3cm/ 5 x 1¼in.

Place on a baking tray, cover with a tea towel and leave to rise for 60 minutes. Preheat the oven to 200°C/400°F/Gas mark 6.

Mix the remaining egg with 1 tablespoon water, then brush the buns with the egg wash. Sprinkle over some sesame seeds and bake in the bottom part of the oven for 20 minutes or until they have turned beautifully brown. Eat on the same day or put in the freezer.

HOW TO MAKE A CEMITA (THE SANDWICH)

If you have got some kind of meat left over, from pulled pork to cochinita pibil, it's a splendid idea to make a cemita - the traditional super-sandwich from Puebla.

4 CEMITAS

4 cemitas (see left)
1 tbsp butter
any leftover barbecue meat, preferably from the West Texas chapter, reheated
1 avocado, peeled, stoned and sliced
pickled red onions (see p.106)
125g/4oz mozzarella, crumbled
smoky tomato salsa (see p.114)

Cut the buns in half and fry the cut surface in a pan with some butter until nice and crispy. Place the reheated meat, sliced avocado, pickled onion, crumbled mozzarella and salsa on the bottom half of the bun. Put the other half on top and enjoy.

PICKLES

Pickles and barbecue fit together like love and kisses. Put them in sandwiches or in salads to add heat, acidity and crunch, or munch them down whole to cheer up your mouth while you're waiting for the next bit of meat.

DILL PICKLES

A simple pickled cucumber is a must for a barbecue. This is how to do it.

2 LARGE JARS

2 tbsp salt
500ml/18fl oz/generous 2 cups white wine
  vinegar
1kg/2¼lb small cucumbers
2 bunches of fresh dill
5 garlic cloves

Boil 500ml/18fl oz/generous 2 cups water, the salt and vinegar together. Place the whole cucumbers in a clean jar with a tight-fitting lid with the dill and garlic cloves and pour over the brine. Tap the jar a little to get rid of the air bubbles. Close the lid. Leave to cool before placing it in the fridge. Ready to eat the day after.

PICKLED OKRA

If you pickle okra (ladies' fingers), they don't get that slightly slimy texture and instead you will end up with a perfectly crunchy snack.

SERVES 6

200g/7oz okra (ladies' fingers)
2 garlic cloves, sliced
1 bunch of fresh dill
1 fresh chilli, eg medium-hot chilli
  or jalapeño
150ml/5fl oz/⅔ cup cider vinegar
½ tsp chilli (chile) flakes
½ tsp salt

Trim the okra by cutting off the stalks together with about ½cm/¼in of the actual flesh. Place them in a nice jar with a tight-fitting lid together with the garlic, the whole bunch of dill and a chilli cut in half. Bring the vinegar and spices to the boil and pour over the okra. Top up with some water if necessary and close the lid. Place the jar in simmering water for 15 minutes, the water doesn't have to cover the whole jar. Once cooled, leave in the fridge at least overnight before you get munching.

HOT CAULIFLOWER

Hot cauliflower might sound like paradox but the hated veg of childhood actually gets quite sexy when you prepare it in this way.

1 JAR

½ cauliflower
4 garlic cloves, sliced
4 fresh chillies, eg medium-hot chillies
  or jalapeño, halved
1 tsp whole black peppercorns
1 tsp chilli (chile) flakes
500ml/18fl oz/generous 2 cups cider
  vinegar
50g/2oz/¼ cup granulated sugar
1 tbsp salt
½ tsp ground cumin
½ tsp dried coriander leaves
½ tsp turmeric

Cut the cauliflower into small florets and slice fairly thinly. Put into a jar with tight-fitting lid together with sliced garlic, halved chillies, peppercorns and chilli flakes. Bring the vinegar, 200ml/7fl oz/generous ¾ cup water, sugar, salt and spices to the boil and pour over the cauliflower. Close the lid. Leave in the fridge at least overnight.

SIMPLE PICKLED JALAPEÑOS
Super-simple snack that you can do using pretty much any kind of chilli.

1 JAR

500ml/18fl oz/generous 2 cups white wine vinegar
2 tbsp salt
400g/14oz fresh chillies, eg medium-hot chillies or jalapeño

Boil 500ml/18fl oz/generous 2 cups water, the vinegar and salt together. Place the whole chillies in a nice jar with a tight-fitting lid and pour over the brine. Tap the jar a little to get rid of the air bubbles. Close the lid. Place the jar in simmering water for 10 minutes, the water doesn't have to cover the whole jar. Leave to cool and put in the fridge. You will get the best results if you wait for a week before eating them.

PICKLED RED ONIONS
This variety of the classic taco condiment is a bit fruitier than normal and will turn a lovely pink colour when pickled.

1 JAR

150ml/5fl oz/⅔ cup freshly squeezed lime
150ml/5fl oz/⅔ cup orange juice
1 tbsp granulated sugar
1 tbsp salt
2 red onions, thinly sliced

Mix the lime and orange juices together with the sugar and salt. Pour into a nice jar with tight-fitting lid together with thinly sliced onion. Close the lid and leave in the fridge overnight. Eat with everything.

PICKLED CARAMELISED ONION
Sweet-sour onion goo - perfect for sandwiches.

SERVES 4

2 red onions, sliced
1 tbsp butter
5 tbsp red wine vinegar
2 tbsp sugar
salt and freshly ground black pepper

Sauté the onion in the butter over a medium heat until soft, about 10 minutes. Add the vinegar and sugar, and fry for another minute. Season with salt and pepper to taste. Put in a sandwich straight away or in a jar, warming it up before eating.

PICKLED WATERMELON RIND

1 JAR

½ watermelon
200ml/7fl oz/generous ¾ cup cider vinegar
200ml/7fl oz/generous ¾ cup water
200ml/7fl oz/1 cup granulated sugar
1 tbsp salt
8 whole black peppercorns
1 cinnamon stick
2 bay leaves

Peel off the green skin from the melon and eat everything except 2cm/¾ in of the pink fruit flesh. You will now have a watermelon rind made up of about half yellow-green and half pink. Cut the melon into 3-4cm/1¼ - 1½ in pieces. Bring the rest of the ingredients to the boil, add the melon and simmer for about 1 minute. Put everything into a nice jar, close the lid and place it in the fridge.

The beautiful grill platter with the essential pickled cucumber at City Market in Luling, Texas.

NEVER FORGET!

CHEESY
STUFF

Normal cheese is nice, but melted cheese is actually fantastically tasty. And even though barbecued meat already is quite fatty, cheese still holds a place among our barbecue sides. I mean, let the one who's never had a hangover cast the first stone.

CHILE CON QUESO

The half-made variety of this dish has made the Texas cuisine simultaneously famous and infamous. However, if you make it yourself, you'll understand how tasty it actually can be.

SERVES 6

1 tbsp butter
½ brown onion, chopped
2 garlic cloves, finely chopped
3-4 fresh chillies, eg medium-hot chillies or jalapeño (it should be hot), sliced
½ tbsp plain (all-purpose) flour
100ml/3½fl oz/scant ½ cup milk
½ tsp turmeric (optional)
about 150g/5oz/1⅓ cups grated Gruyère cheese
about 150g/5oz/1⅓ cups grated mild Cheddar cheese
1 bunch of fresh coriander (cilantro), finely chopped
6 cherry tomatoes, finely diced
100ml/3½fl oz/scant ½ cup crème fraîche
salt

Melt the butter over a medium heat and sauté the onion for a few minutes before adding the garlic and chilli. Sauté for a few more minutes. Stir in the flour and sauté for about a minute, then add the milk and leave to thicken. If you'd like your cheese sauce to have that same lovely yellow colour as real Tex-Mex queso, add the turmeric. Reduce the heat to low and add a little bit of the grated cheese at a time, imagine you are making a cooler version of risotto. When all the cheese has melted, add the coriander (cilantro) and tomatoes, and stir in the crème fraîche. Season with salt and start

dipping immediately. If you leave the sauce over the heat for too long it will start to split. Serve with fried corn tortilla crisps (see p.115).

TEX-MEX MAC'N'CHEESE

A good mac 'n' cheese should be creamy, smooth and tasty – not dry and boring.

SERVES 6

1 tbsp butter
½ brown onion
2 garlic cloves
3-4 fresh chillies, eg medium-hot chillies or jalapeño (it should be hot)
½ tbsp plain (all-purpose) flour
100ml/3½fl oz/scant ½ cup milk
about 150g/5oz/1⅓ cups grated Gruyère cheese
about 150g/5oz/1⅓ cups grated mild Cheddar cheese
1 bunch of fresh coriander (cilantro)
6 cherry tomatoes
100ml/3½fl oz/scant ½ cup crème fraîche
salt
500g/1lb 2oz penne pasta
breadcrumbs, for sprinkling

Follow the instructions for chile con queso (see opposite) – but stop just at the point where you would dip your crisps into the cheese. Instead pour the cheese sauce over freshly boiled pasta, then place in a large ovenproof dish, sprinkle with breadcrumbs, and bake in the oven preheated to the maximum temperature until the surface has gone crispy. Please do regard this recipe as a starting point for your own experiments. A mac 'n' cheese can be flavoured in (almost) any possible way.

BEANS

The Tex-Mex guru Robb Walsh has called beans 'the mashed potato of Texas', and they use it for everything: sandwiches, tacos, barbecue sides, hair masks. Very often, however, your beans will be served in a sweet barbecue sauce – but I don't like that – so instead we'll turn to Mexico for inspiration in this instance.

FRIJOLES REFRITOS

Creamy, mashed beans that can be served with rice, grilled meat, as a dip, and with pretty much any kind of taco or sandwich there is. Think of it like a kind of Mexican hummus.

SERVES 8

500g/1lb 2oz/scant 3 cups dried pinto or
    borlotti beans
150g/5oz pork belly (side), fat rind removed
1 brown onion, halved, one half finely chopped
1 garlic clove, finely chopped
salt

Soak the dried beans in double the amount of water for about 10 hours. Drain and rinse the beans, then place in a large pan and pour in enough fresh water to cover the beans. Add the pork belly (side) and half the onion, then bring to the boil. Reduce the heat and simmer for about 1 hour. Remove the meat and save it for later, discard the onion, and drain off all but about 150ml/5fl oz/2/3 cup of the water. Dice the pork and fry it in a frying pan (skillet), then add the garlic, the finely chopped onion and, towards the end, the beans. Pour over some of the reserved water, mash and continue adding the water until you get a creamy, but not runny, texture. Season with salt to taste.

FRIJOLES DE OLLA

Wonderful Mexican bean casserole. Eat with wheat tortillas or as a side.

SERVES 8

500g/1lb 2oz/scant 3 cups dried pinto or
    borlotti beans
150g/5oz pork belly (side), fat rind removed
1 brown onion, halved, one half finely chopped
1 garlic clove, finely chopped
100ml/3½fl oz/scant ½ cup bitter
salt
½-1 bunch of fresh coriander (cilantro), chopped
125g/4oz mozzarella, cut into strips
100ml/3½fl oz/scant ½ cup crème fraîche
16 fresh pimiento de Padrón, grilled
salt flakes

Soak the dried beans in double the amount of water for about 10 hours. Drain and rinse the beans, then place in a large pan and pour in enough fresh water to cover the beans. Add the pork belly (side) and half the onion, and simmer for about 35 minutes. Remove the meat, dice and fry it in a frying pan (skillet). Add the garlic, the finely chopped onion and, towards the end, the beans. Pour in the bitter and simmer for 10 minutes. Season with salt. Garnish with chopped coriander, strips of mozzarella and a dollop of crème fraîche. Finish off with a bunch of grilled pimento de Padrón (which actually came from Mexico) and sprinkle salt flakes on top.

HOW TO MAKE A MOLLETE

Mollete is a kind of Mexican bruschetta that is perfect to throw together if you have some left-over beans. Just spread beans on a slice of sour-dough bread, top with grated Gruyère, or other cheese that's good for melting, and grill in the oven (or on a barbecue grill). When the cheese has melted, remove and garnish with a fresh tomato salsa made from tomato, coriander (cilantro), chillies, (eg jalapeño), red onion, salt and a squeeze of lime. Delicious.

SALADS & GREENS

It might not be something you'd get served in a barbecue restaurant, but a big, lovely salad is a side that's hard to beat when it's time for a barbecue party.

WATERMELON SALAD

Sweet, cucumbery watermelon is perfectly suited for salad material – especially if you sneak in some sweet-sour pickles.

SERVES 6

½ watermelon
100ml/3½ fl oz pickled watermelon rind
   (see p.106)
½ fennel bulb, shaved
½ red onion. finely sliced
1 fresh chilli, eg medium-hot chilli or
   jalapeño, sliced
1 bunch of fresh mint, finely chopped
1 lime
2 tbsp olive oil
150g/5oz hard goat's cheese, grated
salt and freshly ground black pepper

Dice the watermelon and mix with pickled watermelon rind, the fennel, red onion, chilli and mint. Squeeze over some lime juice, add a dash of oil, then sprinkle the grated cheese on top, and season to taste with salt and pepper.

CUCUMBER SALAD

A simple cucumber salad that adds a well-needed acidity, sweetness, crunch and freshness.

SERVES 6

100ml/3½ fl oz/scant ½ cup cider vinegar
50g/2oz/¼ cup granulated sugar
1½ tsp salt
2 cucumbers, sliced
4 salad onions, sliced
freshly ground black pepper

Mix the vinegar, sugar and salt together until the sugar and salt have dissolved. Stir in the sliced cucumber and finish off with the sliced salad onions and pepper.

CRISPY BRUSSELS SPROUTS

A crunchy, tasty Brussels sprout salad, light years away from those boiled, mushy, gas-smelling things you get at Christmas.

SERVES 6

500g/1lb 2oz Brussels sprouts
3 tbsp olive oil
salt
1 carrot
juice of 1 lime
2 tbsp honey
1 garlic clove, crushed
1 salad onion, finely chopped
2 fresh chillies, eg medium-hot chillies or
   jalapeño, finely sliced
1 bunch of fresh coriander (cilantro),
   finely chopped
1 bunch of fresh mint, finely chopped

Cut the sprouts in half, dip in oil, sprinkle with salt and grill in the oven (or a grill prepared for indirect cooking) for 30 minutes at 175°C/347°F, or until soft inside and crispy on the outside (just like me). For the dressing, julienne (Google it!) or, a bit less cool, grate the carrot and mix with the lime juice, honey and crushed garlic. Stir in the sprouts, check the seasoning, and garnish with the salad onion, chillies, coriander (cilantro) and mint.

SALSAS

If you have the grill going anyway, then why on earth would you not take the opportunity to make a salsa too? No, exactly. Like with any other dishes, the salsas will get even sweeter, tastier and cosier if you leave them to cook on the grill first. Let the dipping begin!

SMOKY TOMATO SALSA
This is the basic salsa that is a must for everyone with a grill and over 5,000 taste buds.

SERVES 6

5 large tomatoes
1 red onion
1-2 fresh chillies, eg medium-hot chillies
    or jalapeño
2 garlic cloves
1 tbsp sherry vinegar
1 lime
1 bunch of fresh coriander (cilantro)
salt

Place the tomatoes, onion, chillies and garlic in an ovenproof dish and leave on the grill while smoking something else until the vegetables have turned a nice colour and seem soft. Blitz in a blender with the vinegar, freshly squeezed lime juice and the coriander (cilantro). Season with salt.

GRILLED TOMATILLO SALSA
Tomatillos are always a treat – but they will get an extra sweet, smoky flavour on the grill.

SERVES 6

200g/7oz tomatillos or physalis (Cape
    gooseberries), halved
2 garlic cloves
½ white onion
1 fresh green chilli, eg medium-hot chilli
    or jalapeño
1 bunch of fresh coriander (cilantro)
salt
granulated sugar (optional)

Grill the halved tomatillos over direct heat for 2 minutes on each side, or until you have some nice grilling stripes going on. Put in a blender with the garlic, onion, chilli and coriander (cilantro), and blend until smooth. Add some water if it gets too chunky. Season with salt and sugar (if it's too sour).

GRILLED PINEAPPLE SALSA
You think fruit salsas are for sissies? Try this and ring me up after.

SERVES 6

½ pineapple, peeled and cut into slices,
    about 1cm/½in thick
½ red onion, finely chopped
½-1 fresh chilli, eg habañero, finely chopped
1 bunch of fresh coriander (cilantro),
    finely chopped
1 lime
salt

Grill the pineapple slices over direct heat for 2 minutes on each side or until nice grill stripes appear. Leave to cool. Chop and mix with the onion, chilli and coriander (cilantro). Squeeze over the lime juice and season with salt.

HOW TO MAKE YOUR OWN TORTILLA CRISPS

It's super-easy to make your own, record-breakingly crispy tortilla crisps: just buy some corn tortillas and cut into 4 portions. Heat enough oil for deep-frying to 175°C/347°F, then deep-fry the tortillas until crispy. Leave to drain on a piece of kitchen paper, then sprinkle with salt and get snacking.

SLAWS

Even though the cabbage, which is the harder cousin of the lettuce, is a perfect match for barbecues, you don't have to use it in your slaw. In fact, most things that are crispy and fresh can be finely shredded and used as a sandwich filling or as a side. Here are a few of my favourites.

CLASSIC COLESLAW
Because sometimes a creamy classic tastes the best.

SERVES 6

½ (about 500g/1lb 2oz) white cabbage, finely shredded
¼ (about 250g/9oz) red cabbage, finely shredded
4 carrots, finely sliced
1 bunch of fresh parsley, finely chopped
200g/7oz/generous ¾ cup mayonnaise
2 tbsp Dijon mustard
2 tbsp wholegrain Dijon mustard
2 tbsp cider vinegar
salt and freshly ground black pepper

Mix the cabbage and carrots together in a bowl, then add the parsley. Make a dressing by mixing the mayonnaise, mustards and vinegar together. Stir into the vegetables and season to taste with salt and pepper.

CAROLINA COLESLAW
Sour and crispy South-state slaw without mayonnaise.

SERVES 8

½ (about 500g/1lb 2oz) white or red cabbage, finely shredded
3 carrots, finely sliced
2 salad onions, finely sliced
200ml/7fl oz/generous ¾ cup cider vinegar
3 tbsp oil
1 tbsp granulated sugar
1½ tsp celery or fennel seeds
salt and freshly ground black pepper

Mix the cabbage, carrots and salad onions together in a bowl. Make a dressing by mixing the vinegar, oil and sugar together. Toast the celery or fennel seeds in a dry pan, then stir into the vegetables and season to taste with salt and pepper.

APPLE SLAW
Beautifully green, crispy slaw. Goes with everything.

SERVES 6

3 tbsp olive oil
2½ tbsp cider vinegar
2 tsp freshly squeezed lemon juice
½ tsp granulated sugar
3 celery stalks
2 green apples
1 fennel bulb
salt and freshly ground black pepper

Whisk the oil, vinegar, lemon juice and sugar together. Julienne (Google it!) the celery and apple, then finely slice the fennel. Mix everything together and season with salt and pepper.

CRISPY GREENS

Vegetables are healthy and tasty, sure, but sometimes you will have to help nature on its way a little to really maximise the crunch.

CRISPY GREEN BEANS
Unhealthy veg? Or healthy chips?

SERVES 6

150ml/5fl oz/⅔ cup pale ale
100g/3½ oz/¾ cup plain (all-purpose) flour
salt
2 tbsp cornflour (cornstarch)
oil, for deep-frying
400g/14oz green beans

Whisk the beer, flour, ½ teaspoon salt and cornflour (cornstarch) together in a bowl and leave to rest for 10 minutes. Heat the oil for deep-frying to 175°C/347°F. Dip the beans into the batter and deep-fry in the oil for 3 minutes or until crispy. Leave to drain on a piece of kitchen paper then season with salt.

CRISPY GREEN TOMATOES'N'CHEESE
An American mozzarella salad.

SERVES 4

oil, for deep-frying
2 beef (beefsteak) tomatoes, as unripe as possible
100g/3½ oz/¾ cup plain (all-purpose) flour
1 egg
100g/3½ oz/¾ cup panko breadcrumbs
salt and freshly ground black pepper
125g/4oz buffalo mozzarella, grated
2 fresh chillies, eg medium-hot chillies or jalapeño, thinly sliced
½ bunch of coriander (cilantro), finely chopped
4 lime wedges

Heat the oil for deep-frying to 175°C/347°F. Slice the tomatoes into 1cm/½ in thick slices and roll them in the flour, egg and then the panko breadcrumbs. Deep-fry in the oil for about 2 minutes on each side or until the panko has turned golden brown. Leave to drain on a piece of kitchen paper. Sprinkle with salt and pepper. Top with the grated mozzarella, chillies and coriander (cilantro). Squeeze over the limes and serve.

SUPER-CRISPY ONION RINGS
Record-breakingly crispy and record-breakingly oniony.

SERVES 8

100g/3½ oz/¾ cup plain (all-purpose) flour
50g/2oz/generous ⅓ cup cornflour (cornstarch)
2 tbsp instant mash powder
½ tsp cayenne pepper
200ml/7fl oz/generous ¾ cup sparkling water
oil, for deep-frying
2-4 brown onions
200g/7oz/scant 1½ cups panko breadcrumbs
salt

Mix the flour, cornflour (cornstarch), instant mash powder and cayenne together in a bowl. Add the sparkling water and stir to make a batter. Leave to thicken. Heat the oil for deep-frying to 175°C/347°F. Slice the onions into ½cm/¼in thick slices and separate into rings. Dip the rings first in the batter then roll in the panko breadcrumbs. Deep-fry in the oil until the rings are golden brown, then leave to drain on kitchen paper.

POTATOES

Meat and potatoes fit together like, well, meat and potatoes. In fact, I don't think I've ever met a potato I haven't liked. I enjoy them in any shape or form there is: oven-baked, boiled, deep-fried and in its liquid form – and in the latter case preferably together with some Kahlua and a dash of ice-cold milk.

TEX-MEX POTATO SALAD
A beautifully red-hot potato salad. A favourite.

SERVES 6

1kg/2¼ lb potatoes
2 tbsp olive oil
salt and freshly ground black pepper
2 red pointed peppers
2 fresh red chillies
1 whole garlic head
2 tbsp mayonnaise
½ tsp ground cumin
1 tsp Spanish paprika
2 salad onions, chopped
fresh parsley, chopped, to garnish
fresh coriander (cilantro), chopped, to garnish
1 lime

Preheat the oven to 225°C/437°F/Gas mark 7. Scrub the potatoes thoroughly and cut into pieces large enough to fit on a fork. Roast in the oven in the oil until nice and crispy, about 20-30 minutes. Season with salt and pepper. Grill the pointed peppers, chilli and whole garlic until the skin goes black and sooty. Put in a plastic bag and wait for 10 minutes before pulling off the skin and removing the stalk and seeds. Squeeze out the garlic cloves. Blend the vegetables with the mayonnaise, cumin and paprika into a smooth dressing. Mix the potatoes in the dressing and stir in the salad onions. Garnish with the chopped parsley and coriander. Squeeze over the lime and serve.

OLD-TIMER POTATO SALAD
A classic super-yummy barbecue side.

SERVES 6

1kg/2¼ lb potatoes
2 tbsp olive oil
salt and freshly ground black pepper
100g/3½ oz/scant ½ cup mayonnaise
50ml/2fl oz/scant ¼ cup pickle juice
1½ tbsp Dijon mustard
2 salad onions, chopped
½ bunch of fresh parsley, chopped
2 celery stalks, chopped
100g/3½ oz finely chopped pickles
   of your choice

Preheat the oven to 225°C/437°F/Gas mark 7. Cut the potatoes into pieces large enough to fit on a fork. Drizzle with oil and roast in the oven until crispy, about 20-30 minutes. Sprinkle with salt and pepper. Mix the mayonnaise, pickle juice and mustard together, and check the seasoning. Mix the potato in the dressing, stir in the salad onions, parsley, celery and pickles, and serve.

SMOKY POTATO CHIPS
Have you ever tried to make your own potato crisps? It's not worth it. With one exception of course: these smoked little goodies.

SERVES 4

100g/3½ oz/⅔ cup salt flakes
aluminium roasting tray

3 baking potatoes
mesquite or hickory wood smoking chips
1 tsp cayenne pepper
1 tsp paprika
½ tsp granulated sugar
½ tsp garlic powder
½ tsp ground cumin
oil, for deep-frying

Make the smoked salt by putting the salt flakes into an aluminium roasting tray and smoking it at 225°C/437°F for about 1 hour using indirect heat. Even if you won't use all the salt now (god forbid), make a proper batch and store in an airtight container for those long grill-free winter nights. Peel and slice the potatoes as thinly as possible, preferably by using a mandoline. No, actually you will have to use a mandoline – or they are guaranteed to end up too thick. Place the potato slices in a bowl filled with ice-cold water for 30 minutes and after that: leave them for at least 1 hour to dry off on a piece of kitchen paper (paper towels), flipping them over halfway through. Mix the spices with 1 tablespoon of the smoked salt. Heat the oil for deep-frying to 175°C/347°F. Deep-fry the potatoes in the oil, a couple at a time, until they have turned a nice colour and seem crispy. Leave to drain on kitchen paper, then sprinkle with the spice mix and eat.

SHOESTRING FRIES

In the summer, you might not fancy standing in the kitchen and making triple-fried chips all the time. That's when these thin, crispy shoestring fries are perfect, as one round in the chip pan is all they need.

SERVES 4

2 tbsp salt
1–2 tbsp finely chopped fresh coriander (cilantro)
zest of 1 lime

500g/1lb 2oz potatoes
oil, for deep-frying

Crush the salt, coriander (cilantro) and lime zest together using a pestle and mortar – or blend – until the salt has turned a beautiful green colour. If it feels wet to touch, spread the mixture out on a plate and leave to dry for 2 hours. Peel the potatoes and cut into thin matchsticks. Try to pat off some of the starch with kitchen paper (paper towels). Heat the oil for deep-frying to 175°C/347°F, and deep-fry the potatoes in the oil, in batches, until golden brown and crispy. Leave to drain on kitchen paper. Sprinkle with the lime salt and serve immediately.

BAKED SWEET POTATOES

Baked sweet potato tastes smooth and naturally sweet together with other barbecued food. Those with adventurous taste buds can try some maple cinnamon butter to go with it – if not, just butter and salt will also do the trick.

SERVES 6

6 sweet potatoes, scrubbed
foil
salt and freshly ground black pepper

MAPLE CINNAMON BUTTER

6 tbsp butter, at room temperature
½ tbsp maple syrup
½ tsp salt
¼ tsp ground cinnamon

Preheat the oven to 200°C/400°F/Gas mark 6. Wrap the cleaned sweet potatoes in foil and bake in the oven for 45 minutes or until they seem soft. Alternatively, grill them. If you want maple cinnamon butter: mix the butter with the maple syrup, salt and cinnamon. Or don't bother and just eat like normal baked potatoes with butter, salt and pepper.

HOW TO MAKE THE PERFECT GRILLED CORN ON THE COB

Soak the unpeeled corn on the cobs in water. When the charcoal has turned grey, grill the corn until the husk starts to blacken - the corn underneath will be perfectly steamed. Peel off the husk and put the corn back on the grill. Brush with melted butter, sprinkle with salt and grill until they have coloured nicely. In a frying pan (skillet): cut off the raw corn kernels from the cob and fry in a little butter until they seem roasted.

CORN ON THE COB

Everyone knows that corn + fire = yum. So here are three suggestions for how to serve the cobs, plus a foolproof method of preparing them. If you carefully steam the corn in its own husk before grilling, you will get a perfect result every time, plus a lovely smoky flavour.

ELOTES
Mexican grilled corn.

SERVES 4

4 fresh corn on the cobs with husk
1 tbsp butter
salt
3 tbsp mayonnaise
4 tbsp grated Manchego cheese
1 tsp chilli powder
1 lime

Grill the corn according to the instructions on the left (this is the step where you will use the butter and the salt). When the cobs are done, brush them with the mayonnaise and roll them in the cheese. Sprinkle with chilli powder and add a squeeze of lime.

BOURBON CREAMED CORN
Creamy corn with a sting of whisky.

SERVES 6–8

5 fresh corn on the cobs with husk
1 tbsp butter
salt
4 shallots, finely chopped
3 garlic cloves, finely chopped
50g/2oz/4 tbsp butter
2 fresh chillies, eg medium-hot chillies or jalapeño, finely chopped
150ml/5fl oz/⅔ cup whipping or double (heavy) cream
1-2 tbsp bourbon
4 salad onions, finely chopped

Grill the corn according to the instructions on the left (this is the step where you will use the 1 tablespoon of butter and the salt). Fry the shallots and garlic in the 50g/2oz/4 tbsp butter over a medium heat until they start to soften. Add the chillies, cream and bourbon. Cut off the corn kernels from the grilled cobs and add to the pan. Leave to simmer until everything is nice and creamy. Season with salt and garnish with the salad onions.

ESQUITES
Mexican grilled corn salad.

SERVES 4

4 fresh corn on the cobs with husk
1 tbsp butter
salt
1 fresh chilli (chile), eg medium-hot chilli or jalapeño, finely chopped
1 garlic clove, finely chopped
½ bunch of fresh coriander (cilantro), finely chopped
3 tbsp mayonnaise
½-1 lime
1 salad onion, finely chopped
2 tbsp grated Manchego cheese

Grill the corn according to the instructions on the left (this is the step where you will use the butter and the salt). For the dressing, mix the chilli, garlic and coriander (cilantro) with the mayonnaise and freshly squeezed lime juice. Cut off the corn kernels from the grilled cob and mix with the dressing. Sprinkle over the salad onion and grated cheese.

TRIP

A STICKY-SAUCE FAMILY TRIP THROUGH TEXAS

It's one of those things you always start planning when under the influence of alcohol. 'I know what we should do,' your friend will say when the topic is brought up. 'We should buy a car in New York, a nice old American one, then we will sell it when we reach Los Angeles. That way the trip won't cost us a penny.'

'Oh, just imagine leaving everything behind,' you will say in a dreaming voice and before your eyes you will see yourself standing in some desert with a map folded out over the bonnet of a dusty Cadillac.

In your fantasy, you are wearing pilot glasses, a Hawaiian shirt and look a bit like either Michael Madsen or Winona Ryder.

'Let's just do it,' your friend says. 'Tomorrow we'll book the flight.'

'Yes, let's do it,' you reply enthusiastically. 'And this time it's not just something we say.'

Then you shake hands, order in another round of beers, and the next day, of course, you won't hear from each other. Instead you're both suffering from a hangover, each in his or her own place, eating cheesecake and watching TV reruns.

Competing with starting a diving school in Phuket or opening a sourdough bakery by the sea, a roadtrip through America could be the most common non-executed dream in the world. But it doesn't have to be like that. Because in comparison to most other ideas you will get at 2.30am, going on a roadtrip isn't just an idea, it's a fantastic idea. It's something you'll just have to do. I would even go as far as saying that each and everyone should, at some point in life, go on a long roadtrip through the US.

Personally, I have been on seven, eight shorter and longer roadtrips. But four years ago I became a dad, and since then it's mostly just been package holidays. This is because everything that used to take

about five minutes – eat, go to the toilet, get dressed – takes about two hours when you have kids and is so tiring that only one small thing going wrong, like the child complaining about a lumpy sock, could make the whole system break apart and me ending up sobbingly threatening to cancel Friday night TV. So the mere thought of stuffing everything you will need into a car and having to pack and unpack every day soon turned so absurd that my partner and I started to spend our travel budget on family-friendly holiday resorts with pool areas, travel guide performances and grown-up angst.

Although I'd never stopped dreaming about roadtrips altogether, I had simply rejected them as a non-realistic holiday option. That is until one day I needed something to read on the toilet and, by chance, picked up John Steinbeck's classic travel story *Travels with Charley* – a book about the Nobel Prize-winning author's 10,000-mile-long roadtrip across the US in his campervan Rocinante together with his poodle Charley. I opened it and read the first paragraph of the first page:

'When I was very young and the urge to be someplace else was on me, I was assured by mature people that maturity would cure this itch. When years described me as mature, the remedy prescribed was middle age. In middle age I was assured that greater age would calm my fever and now that I am fifty-eight perhaps senility will do the job. Nothing has worked. Four hoarse blasts of a ship's whistle still raise the hair on my neck and set my feet to tapping. The sound of a jet, an engine warming up, even the clopping of shod hooves on pavement brings on the ancient shudder, the dry mouth and vacant eye. ... In other words ... once a bum always a bum. I fear this disease is incurable.'

Excited, I ran out to my partner and read

the piece aloud and after she told me to pull up my pants she said: 'John Steinbeck is right. It's time to go on a roadtrip again.'

I spent the next few days in front of the computer. I Googled, looked at maps and listened exclusively to songs about telling your boss to f**k off and just leaving.

'We don't need no destination. Just a tank of gas and a good, clear station', Darryl Worley sang in *A Good Day to Run* and I sat in front of the computer and nodded along with the music as if I were agreeing with everything he said.

But of course I didn't. Because instead every hotel was soon booked, every stretch of road measured and every meal planned. This time, we wouldn't go on a super-long round trip, but instead stick to the state that would give us the absolute most bang for the buck: Texas. Instead of letting the sights or chance decide our route, we would travel between the state's best barbecue joints. The reason for this was, of course, that barbecue is tasty. But also because I knew from earlier visits that these were simple, rustic places where (probably) it wouldn't be an embarrassment to bring the one- and four-year-old Somali sea pirates that my daughters were transformed into as soon as we went out for a meal.

'INSTEAD OF LETTING THE SIGHTS OR CHANCE DECIDE OUR ROUTE, WE'D TRAVEL BETWEEN THE STATE'S BEST BARBECUE JOINTS.'

When we eventually landed in Houston and after a night's sleep, we packed ourselves into the rental car and programmed the GPS to take us to Bryan. Bryan is a small town in eastern Texas, famous for its Afro-American barbecue restaurants in general and Fargo's Pit BBQ in particular. It was only just before 11am in America, but 5pm in our stomachs, so when, still a mile away from the town, I could smell the smoke I got so hungry straight away, I started to see barbecue sauce-coloured spots in front of my eyes. When we drove up in front of the simple blue-painted shack on the outskirts of the town, there were a couple of battered pick-ups with the engines still running parked on the street outside, and as soon as the door to the restaurant opened people ran out of the cars with crumpled-up dollar bills in their hands and a craving for barbecue in their eyes. The restaurant wasn't much larger than a country fair stand, and while we were queuing we saw how the staff carried in freshly smoked briskets, ribs, sausages and chickens from the smoker in the courtyard. I ordered a brisket sandwich, took a bite and immediately my whole barbecue life flashed before my eyes: I saw sausages on kettle grills and pre-marinated gammon steaks sizzling away under canopies while the rain was pouring down outside. I saw teenage drunkenness, disposable grills, garden recliners, light beer and how my dad walked over to the grill outside the house I grew up in and, long after we'd eaten, looked at the charcoal and said: 'I see. Now the charcoal is perfect for grilling.'

As if it were the charcoal's or the grill's fault. Or the whole damn world's. I saw – no, felt – all those times I had put a mouthful of grilled meat in my mouth and had been shocked by how good something so simple as meat, cooked with the heat from wood, really could be.

'EVERYONE SHOULD, AT SOME POINT IN LIFE, GO ON A LONGER ROADTRIP THROUGH THE US.'

Yes, the maillard reaction's impact on animal protein really is one of our most basic, powerful taste sensations. Perhaps that's why we continue to eat meat, even though we really shouldn't, and it's probably the reason why the outdoor grill is our upmost debated piece of kitchen equipment (possibly alongside the teppanyaki grill), and why it's likely to be described as a status symbol, class definer or a tool to maintain some kind of gender power structure.

While I munched down the last bit of the brisket sandwich, I did, however, decide to stand up to those patriarchal structures that are likely to automatically place the men in front of the grill. Instead I would, as soon as they have developed some kind of motor skill, teach both of my daughters how to light a grill, rub a piece of meat, cook up a barbecue sauce, and that barbecuing is a pretty good excuse to crack open a beer a couple of hours before anyone else.

This book is for you, girls.

After we'd wiped all the barbecue sauce off the children, we went back to the car to drive to Lockhart – the barbecue capital of the world. Lockhart is the hub for central Texas' distinctive barbecue style and lies about an hour's drive south of Austin – and five hours from Bryan – so of course we had to stop for some barbecue on the way. In the small town of Luling, just outside Lockhart, there's a famous barbecue place called City Market that we decided to try.

City Market turned out to be incorporated, as the name suggests, into a convenience store, and after walking past the newspaper stand, drinks fridges and cough medecines and through a couple of swing doors, you are into a barbecue pit so smoky, hot and dirty it looked like one of hell's most neglected front yards.

It was one of the most beautiful restaurants I've ever seen.

For $11 (£8) we got perfectly barbecued meat for the whole family: brisket, ribs and homemade sausages served on a piece of waxed paper with only white bread, onion and pickles to go with it. The drinks you bought in the convenience store. The traditional barbecue drink in Texas is beer, ice tea or soda – and not the diet variety, as you will get a mad craving for fast carbs after eating so much pure protein. Any kind of soda won't do, however; it should be sweetened by sugar from sugar cane and not corn syrup. Classic choices are, for example, the cinnamon-smelling Texas drink Big Red, the Southern state favourite Dr Pepper or Mexican Coca-Cola, whose bottles are still beautifully screen-printed and contain more natural ingredients. City Market's barbecue was, of course, sublime.

That night, we fell asleep by 7pm, still so full that I dreamed about a machine that made ladies' shoes all night.

The following morning the belly rumbled again and we went to have some breakfast at the classic barbecue joint Smitty's Market. Smitty's is a typical old German meat market from the nineteenth century. The barbecue style in central Texas dates back to when the German immigrants brought their smoked sausages and deli meat to the new country. When you enter the premises, which are permeated by smoke, you see an enormous open fire that gives heat and smoke flavour to a couple of even bigger barbecue pits, from which serious-looking men without any nerve cells in their fingertips take out and cut up ridiculously juicy bits of cow. In the old part, long benches run alongside the walls, still with knives fastened to the school-like tables with chains – a legacy from the times when the barbecue joints weren't visited by Western-romantic Swedish food writers, but by rock-hard ranch workers and short-tempered cowboys.

A stone's throw from Smitty's is Black's BBQ, one of the oldest and nicest-looking barbecue places. My daughter Dixie had ribs large enough to tip over the Flintstone's car and I got a guide around the kitchen.

The next day we were up extra early to start the two-hour drive to the tiny town of Lexington, north of Austin. Because that's where you'll find Snow's BBQ – a place that's been voted Texas' best and that's only open on Saturdays from 8am until the meat has run out (which normally happens around lunchtime). Snow's pitmaster is an older woman named Tootsie Tomanetz, and she was kind enough to show me around her fantastically cool outdoor pit before it was time to start queuing up for food.

If you work as a food writer, people often ask 'what's the nicest thing you've ever eaten?', upon which I normally mumble something and then quickly change the topic since I never know what to answer. But now I know. Because the brisket that Tootsie served that day was the tastiest thing I've ever eaten. It's hard to describe exactly how it tasted – but it was a perfect balance of meat, fat, salt, pepper, smoke and fire. Even though every pitmaster aims for this result every time, it was probably just by pure chance that I got to experience it right there and then. Brisket is recognised as a hard cut of meat to get right, and if you are to succeed perfectly everything has to be correct: the individual piece of meat that's to be cooked, the piece of meat you've been served as a guest, the current state of the smoker, the skill of the pitmaster, the quality of the fire and even the weather all play a part. But when everything is right, it's pure and unadulterated food alchemy. In the evening, we were so tired that we just shared some fruit salad and fell asleep in front of the TV. I did, however, wake up after a couple of hours, jet-lagged and hungry, and decided to sneak out to the diner for an (extremely) early breakfast.

There's not really a European equivalent to the American diner. Even though the diner often is open around the clock and is situated along motorways and junctions, it's wrong to compare them to common road restaurants. Because even in the shabbiest of diners, you can get a perfect burger or a pile of fluffy pancakes with syrup and ridiculously crispy bacon.

Another thing that the diner has but the road restaurant lacks is romance. Sitting by a long bar while a gum-chewing waitress pours you coffee and calls you 'honey' immediately makes you have a tannin-fuelled flashback to all the road movies you've ever seen and, as a result, you will feel about 300 per cent cooler than you really are.

'BECAUSE EVEN IN THE SHABBIEST OF DINERS, YOU CAN GET A PERFECT BURGER OR A PILE OF FLUFFY PANCAKES WITH SYRUP AND RIDICULOUSLY CRISPY BACON.'

A nice democratic core value in the diner culture is also the idea that everyone should be able to eat there. A meal has in fact always been priced at roughly the equivalent of what a low-waged worker earns in an hour and a half. While I sat there and stirred my coffee, a policeman came in and

ordered a cup to go. I gave him a quick nod (and felt about 400 per cent cooler than I really am) and thought that in America the simplest, cheapest food is more than just a way to fill up, it's an ideology. Beyond the horrible chains, there is a fast food culture that is just that, a culture: people discuss, engage with, and fight over which local restaurant serves the best sausage, tastiest sandwich, yummiest burger or the most sublime taco. And in Texas barbecue is more than just food, it's an obsession.

Narrow-minded Europeans might be quick to dismiss Texas as a place for rednecks or conservative George Bush-types. But that's just the same as saying that there are only fishermen in Scotland or crime writers in Sweden. In reality, the state is the second largest in the US and contains most kinds of places – from the most conservative parts in the northeast to the extremely bohemian hippie haunts like Austin or West Texas.

And it was just to West Texas we were heading to next. To prevent the kids from flipping out from boredom, we spread the journey over two days – and were forced to stay one night in a shabby motel in the rough border town Del Rio. The motel was of that kind you have seen in a million romantic road movies and that you dream about staying in – until you actually do. Because in reality they smell of dental surgeries and come with strange lumps underneath the carpet. So instead of spending the night like Alabama and Clarence in *True Romance,* you try to stay as still as possible so you don't accidentally touch the bedspread with your face.

However, in the morning it turned out that the motel served amazing breakfast tacos from a taquería nearby. This is one of the things I really like in this part of the world. When you least expect it, in the filthiest of environments, you can all of a sudden get served a fantastic meal.

The town of Marfa is situated on a 1,400m/4,593 ft high plateau in the Chihuahua desert, a high desert, which means that even though it's hot as hell in the daytime, the temperature creeps down to around 0°C/32°F at night. It's

about a seven-hour car journey from the nearest whatever, and it's that kind of place where the air feels clearer in a way, the atmosphere softer and the light more beautiful. We checked into our mega-cosy trailer and went out to look for barbacoa.

I had heard about the taquería Tacos El Norte, and it turned out to be a proper old-school Mexican which served tacos with genuine cow's head *barbacoa* as well as with *lengua* (cow's tongue). It was rather wonderful. Except that I drank a *horchata* with the food, a sweet Mexican rice drink that is so far the only thing within the Tex-Mex food culture that I have found diffi-

cult to like. Well, difficult – I hated it. Tasted horrendous. Like if someone had mixed a glass of milk with a jar of skin cream.

The morning after, we had some breakfast burritos with wheat tortillas straight out of the oven at Marfa Burritos – a fantastic little place where you bought the food straight out of the owner's kitchen. After that it was time to get on the road again. It was in the Marfa area that films like James Dean's *Giant* and the Coen brothers' *No Country for Old Men* were shot. The countryside is incredibly beautiful and a bit spooky. Not in a million years would we stop to pick up hitchhikers with bowl haircut and captive bold pistols powered by compressed air. After passing the border town of Presidio, we drove through Big Bend until we eventually reached Terlingua Ghost Town – which has been called the most remote place in the US. When we were about to check into the small house we had rented, we couldn't enter at first as a massive, hairy tarantula was basking in the sun just outside the door. After a few moments filled with tears and giggles, a

'WE CHECKED IN TO OUR MEGA-COSY TRAILER AND WENT OUT TO LOOK FOR BARBACOA.'

cowboy passed by and killed it with a stick. I love Texas!

Every year Terlingua hosts the world championships in chilli-making and the bar Starlight Theatres is said to have the best chilli in the world. It was okay. But the beer was cold and there was a nice breeze coming through despite the hot desert night, and when the troubadour said, 'let's send a thought to those sorry bastards who suffer up in the snow, while we sit down here, with open doors and an ice cold beer on the table' it was one of life's most perfect moments.

The absolutely most hyped barbecue place in Texas (and the world) is Franklin BBQ in Austin. Their brisket has been named 'best in the universe', the owner Aaron Franklin is a TV celebrity, and there are long, serious articles written about the rivalry between Franklin BBQ and JM Mueller BBQ (now LA BBQ) in newspapers like the *New York Times*. And just as we thought: when we arrived in Austin just after eleven o'clock on one of the last days of our culinary journey, the queue was already long. After about an hour and a half, we had finally reached the till and could order some brisket, ribs and a pulled pork sandwich. While I chomped down the last brisket of the journey, I was contemplating how easy it had been to go on a roadtrip with two small children – a lot easier, in fact, than taking them to nursery on a normal day. They had been happy all the time, were excited by the same things as us grown-ups (cowboys, massive trucks and stuffed racoons), and as soon as they sat down in their child safety seats they went out quicker than Anton Chigurh's victims in *No Country for Old Men*. I was thinking how a roadtrip is more than a holiday; it's a journey through the pop-cultural landscape that has shaped us.

'I WAS THINKING HOW A ROADTRIP IS MORE THAN A HOLIDAY; IT'S A JOURNEY THROUGH THE POP-CULTURAL LANDSCAPE THAT HAS SHAPED US.'

Every day you make some references to your life. From the apple pie at the diner, that looks exactly like the one Grandma Duck baked for Huey, Dewey and Louie in the Donald Duck cartoons of my youth, to the bar you by chance come across in the middle of the Chihuahua desert that's an exact copy of The Titty Twister in *From Dusk Till Dawn*.

The American countryside is also filled to the brim with the kinds of tourist attractions you're really interested in: instead of some old church built by a boring duke, you drive past the spot where James Dean drove himself to death, the junction where Robert Johnson sold his soul to the devil, or the place where Ham the Astro-chimp is buried. And to discover a new place every day and experience things afresh, is also one of the few ways for us adults to experience how magical life was when we were kids.

Hence, the irony that when we need the roadtrip the most, we can no longer cope to go on it.

INDEX

First published in Great Britain in 2014 by
Pavilion Books
The Old Magistrates Court
10 Southcombe Street
London
W14 0RA

An imprint of the Anova Books Company Ltd

www.anovabooks.com

Commisioning Editor: Emily Preece-Morrison
Assistant Editor: Charlotte Selby
Cover: Georgina Hewitt
Designer: Briony Hartley
Translator: Frida Green
Copy editor: Kathy Steer
Proofreader: Alyson Silverwood

ISBN: 9781909815100

A CIP catalogue record for this book is available from the British Library.

10 9 8 7 6 5 4 3 2 1

Reproduction by Mission Productions Limited, Hong Kong
Printed and bound by 1010 Printing International Limited, China

First published in Sweden in 2012 as
Texas BBQ
by Natur & Kultur, Stockholm

www.nok.se
info@nok.se

© 2013 JONAS CRAMBY
Natur & Kultur, Stockholm
Text and photos: Jonas Cramby
Design: Kristin Lidström
Form: Jonas Cramby
Props: Li Winther
Editor: Maria Nilsson